TRADITION IN JAVANESE SOCIAL STRUCTURE

P.M. LAKSONO

TRADITION
IN JAVANESE SOCIAL STRUCTURE
KINGDOM AND COUNTRYSIDE
Changes in the Javanese Conceptual Model

Translated by:
E.G. Koentjoro

GADJAH MADA UNIVERSITY PRESS
1986

Perpustakaan Nasional: katalog dalam terbitan (KDT)

Laksono, P.M.
    Tradition in Javanese social structure: kingdom and country
side: changes in the Javanese conceptual model/P.M. Laksono;
translated by E.G. Koentjoro. -- Yogyakarta: Gadjah Mada University Press. 1986.
    xxv. 104 hal.: ilus.: 21 cm.
    Judul asli: Tradisi dalam struktur masyarakat Jawa kerajaan
dan pedesaan: alih ubah model berpikir Jawa.
    Bibliografi: hal. 93—104.
    ISBN 979—420—021—2.
    1. Jawa - Keadaan sosial - Abad 18.
    2. Jawa - Keadaan pedesaan.   I. Judul.
II. Kuncoro. E.G.

959.82

Original Edition	: **Tradisi Dalam Struktur Masya-** **rakat Jawa, Kerajaan dan Pede-** **saan; alih ubah model berpikir** **Jawa.**
By	: P.M. Laksono.
English Edition	: **Tradition in Javanese Social** **Structure, Kingdom and Coun-** **tryside; changes in the Javanese** **conceptual model.**

© 1985, GADJAH MADA UNIVERSITY PRESS
P.O. Box 14 Bulaksumur, Yogyakarta,
Indonesia.

233.39.10.86

Printed in Indonesia by:
GADJAH MADA UNIVERSITY PRESS
8609226 — C1E

ISBN 979—420—021—2

For
LUCIA MARIA WIDIASTUTI RAHAYU
AND
ALOYSIUS PUTRA SETYANTO

— One Thousand Days —

FOREWORD

It is a pleasure for me to introduce this book by P.M. Laksono, whom I came to know and highly to appreciate during the years 1981–1983, which he spent at Leiden University for post-graduate training and research. A work with such a rich and varied contents will appeal to various readers in many different ways. In my Foreword I shall not speak of what it has to offer to the Java specialist, as this is beyond my competence. The following notes will discuss the book's interest for present-day anthropological theory, and for a study of the way Indonesian cultures are interrelated, i.e. for Indonesia as a "Field of Anthropological Study" (J.P.B. de Josselin de Jong 1983/1935 particularly as regards the position of the Ruler.

The book's title is enlightening, as it neatly summarizes its principal aspects: "Tradition in Javanese Social Structure: Kingdom and Countryside. (Changes in the Javanese Conceptual Model)." It is clear, therefore, that we shall have to speak of tradition and structure. "It should also be kept in mind that what makes social-structure studies valuable is that structures are models ..." (Lévi-Strauss 1953: 528), and Laksono rightly states that he is dealing with models. These models, he says, are conceptual or cognitive; when we are discussing a book by a Javanese about Javanese cognitive models, it will obviously be important to consider the interrelation between the objective and the subjective model: the concepts of *the* Javanese and the author's "intimate knowledge" of them. The "kingdom", specifically mentioned in the title, directly entails the position of the king, and this topic brings us to the intra-Indonesian comparative approach mentioned above.

If we now consider the book's contents in some detail we see how these themes are interwoven in the consecutive chapters and sections, so that a closely reasoned, compact text results.

In the opening pages of Chapter I, the themes of tradition and structure are already introduced. It is noteworthy that Laksono immediately makes it clear that one needs these concepts for understanding a *changing* society. For example, one has to know whether, when the Dutch introduced the "culture system" *(cultuurstelsel)* to Java this was imposed upon an undifferentiated or a stratified society; and one has to know the "traditions within the social structure" of Bagelen (the region to be discussed more fully in chapter III) precisely because it is a region of great spacial mobility, witness the migrations to the Priangan area. The idea is further developed in chapter I, where the author comes out strongly against popular misconceptions about tradition: "traditional" is not synonymous with "static", and not antithetical to "modern"!

At this point, early in his book, Laksono begins to construct the *model* which, in later sections, he will use for interpreting the Javanese data. He needs such a model because, as we have seen, he needs to discover the *structure* of the society he is studying, and, as Lévi-Strauss has said, social structure is not situated in the empirically observable reality, but in the model of that reality. More preciasely, he is now concerned with his society's *tradition,* and one of the functions of tradition is to stand above very-day reality and to formulate and uphold ideals, rules and aims. Following Heesterman, the author now introduces two of the four basic components of his model: tradition is, on the one hand, *transcendent* (i.e. going beyond actual practice), while it also has to be *immanent,* in the sense of having direct relevance to the changing, "real life" situation. These two aspects of tradition can come into conflict with each other.

In the preface, a personal statement the writer gives his reasons for using hardly any unpublished material-but the modestly refrains from mentioning his personal knowledge. Chapter III in particular deals with Bagelen, the district from which he hails. We shall return presently to the advantages and the problems involved for a writer of a scholarly treatise, particularly in anthropology, who *knows* his subject in this special way.

In Chapter II, section 1, the author, following Soemarsaid moertono, stresses the importance of the position attributed to the Ruler in the state of Mataram and its offshoots, Surakarta and Yogyakarta. For a study of kingship in these central Javanese states the paired concepts of "transcendent" versus "immanent" are joined to the oppositional pair "theoretical" versus "practical" to form a four-cell matrix. We now have the complete model which will serve as a means for analysis and explanation throughout the book.

At first sight the reader may find this model rather daunting, as it seems to be so extremely abstract. However, it is in my opinion one of the merits of the present book that this seemingly abstract model soon proves to be applicable to specific data; in other words, the abstract model makes us understand observed phenomena. A case in point is given in the same section II.1.

To begin with, Mr. Laksono tries to situate Javanese Kingship in his matrix model, which leads to the startling conclusion that it belongs to each of the four cells of the matrix: its features are both immanent and transcendent, both practical and theoretical. (Laksono calls this the "paradox" of Javanese kingship; I would prefer to say that this kingship is ambilavent, and thus represents the totality). Next, he sees this same "paradoxical" or conciliatory feature in other aspects of Javanese society as well. This becomes clear when he compares Java with India. Javanese culture has been greatly influenced by Indian Hinduism, which entailed the caste system; but we then see a fundamental difference between the two societies. The Indian caste system is based on *oppositions,* the most fundamental of which is "pure" versus "impure". However, when Java adopted Indian cultural features it did so selectively, and rejected the caste system based on oppositions in favour, once more, of conciliation. The result is that Javanese culture, while adopting Hinduisme, could not adopt a caste system, and that Javanese society is stratified, but not hierarchical (cp. Dumont 1970). Is this conciliatory, ambivalent-or, to use Laksono's own term, paradoxical- attitude in accordance with the ideas underlying Javanese mythology? This question is answered in the next section (II.2), which deals with "kingship in the *wayang* theatre".

This brings us back to the first of the six principal themes of the book, viz. *tradition;* to be exact, the traditional views of the ruler's position in relation to his subjects. We can learn this view by considering the relation which Semar and his three sons maintain with their masters, the Pandawa. The *punakawan* act as advisers, i.e. in wisdom and insight they are superior to the Pandawa who, as *satria,* are their social superiors. The ideology is one of democracy. Laksono expresses this by using the Javanese phrase *jumbuhing kawula lan gusti,* and this very pregnant phrase (the interaction – or intermingling, or even fusion of Servant and Lord) will serve him as another guide, or model, for the interpretation of the data still to be discussed. In fact, at a higher level the roles of Servant and Lord might even be said to be reversed, as the *punakawan* are actually gods, incarnated on earth clowns and servants in order to fulfill their special mission. This means that Semar is the paradoxial, ambivalent, total figure *par excellence,* so that he occupies the central position in the matrix model, where the four cells meet.

In Figure 3 of section II.2 and the accompanying text, the author therefore introduces three notable modifications[1]. In the

Notes

1) Some readers may at first have difficulty in reading Figure 3, as in this diagram each whole side of the square represents a concept, and the opposite sides in consequence stand for opposed concepts. Another more frequently adopted convention is to express the oppositions by dividing the sides of the square in half. Without altering the meaning, we could represent Figure 4 according to this convention.

	Transcendent	Immanent
Theoretical, essential	I	II
Practical, existential	IV	III

first place the importance of the central point is stressed. Second-
ly, from here onwards, the terms "essential" and "exixtential"
(very prominent as technical terms in philosophy) will be employed besides, or instead of, "theoretical" and "practical", res-
pectively. In the third place the model can now also be applied diachronically: human life, and the course of events in *lakon*, moves
from the supernatural cells I and II to the natural, material and
daily events of cells III and IV, and through them back to the supernatural sphere of I. The immobile centre of this movement is
the "paradoxical" unity of Servant and Lord. It is this unifying
point, which reconciles all oppositions, which Laksono defines as
typical for Javanese thinking.

It is this passage, in section II.2, which makes the greatest
demands on the reader's concentration and understanding, so he
will be advised to follow Laksono's explanations with attention. If
he does so, he will find that this passage clarifies the reasoning of
all subsequent sections. For our purpose it is appropriate to note
that here, again, three basic features of Laksono's study are interwoven: *tradition* in Javanese cultures (here apparent in the
wayang theatre), the use of an explanatory *model* for studying it,
and the accent on kingship: from now on, the *ruler* becomes a
most important element in the exposé. We see this clearly in
the two final sections of chapter II.

Section II.3 continues the discussion of the Unity of Servant
and Lord, but again with new features introduced into the analysis: the concept of the Ideal King, and the ruler's *kasekten*, which
may be rendered in English as mystic and sacral power, acquired
by asceticism.

The ideal king is indispensable for a study like Laksono's,
which is so much concerned with cognition, i.e. the manner in
which a society perceives – or wishes to perceive – itself, its environment and its goverment. However, the author immediately
adds the cautionary note that reality is often far from the ideal.
This is more than a truism: it clearly shows that the author, in spite of the consistency with which he applies his model, is far from

being a "model-maniac" – a reproach so often made to scholars who favour structural anthropology.

In one of the first sentences of this Foreword we mentioned the services which Laksono's book renders, implicitly rather than explicitly, to a type study carried out particularly by Indonesianist anthropologists at Leiden University: intra-Indonesian comparative studies or, in other words, the effort to consider Indonesia as a whole as a Field of Anthropological Study (conveniently abbreviated as FAS). As the present book was almost entirely written while the author was a post-graduate researcher at Leiden, we may be permitted to add a few words on this topic.

A number of recent and forthcoming publications by members of the FAS group (e.g. P.E. de Josselin de Jong 1980; R.E. Jordaan and P.E. de Josselin de Jong, forthcoming) deal with the way in which the ruler is portrayed by myths and historiographies in Indonesian literature, and in particular with the way kingship is legitimated. This leads to a study of the depicted relation between ruler and realm, king and subjects. This proves to be very ambiguous – or, as Laksono would probably call it, "paradoxical". It will be clear that when Laksono accentuates the coming together of Servant and Lord he is, on the one hand, thinking along the same lines as his Leiden colleagues, but is also, as a Javanist, adding a new dimension of depth to this on-going research project.

The same applies to his passages on the Javanese ruler's mystic, sacral power. This power, he says, "is particularly required in situations of crisis, due to an external (or even supernatural) threat". As an example he quotes the *Babad Tanah Djawi's* description of the volcanic eruption of the Merapi in 1672: "Only when the king had commanded the learned *(ulama* and *haji)* to pray to Allah did Merapi's anger subside". The reader will not wish to be a merely passive reader of this passage. It will stimulate him to consider similar cases in other works; let us take the Malay Annals, for instance. When the Portuguese launch their attack on malacca, Sultan Ahmad turns to religious exercises. The Annalist – no admirer of Ahmad – deals with this episode in ironical tones:

"This is not the time to study the Unity of Allah!" (Brown 1952: 167, 168), but do we not now begin to see its hidden meaning? Thanks to Laksono, the *Babad Tanah Jawi* can help to elucidate the *Sejarah Melayu* in the FAS context!

Many more examples could be given of this book's value for cross-cultural purposes. For the sake of brevity, I shall only mention two. The formation of a *new* dynasty by means of a "revitalizing marriage", which Laksono notes as a *babad* theme also occupied the two Leiden authors just mentioned; and the *Babad Tanah Djawi's* concern with the significance of dates *(sengkala)* immediately suggests the role of numerology in various other Indonesian cultures, e.g. in Malay-language law books (see Moyer 1975).

We have been speaking of Laksono's research as a stimulus for the actively co-operative reader. At this point we should mention Laksono as not only a researcher, but also a participant member of the society he is studying; that is to say, we must give due attention to his "intimate knowledge". This appears very clearly in the conclusions to section II.3. which can be briefly summarized as follows.

The issue is, what legitimates a Javanese ruler; the author emphatically states that legitimation *(pembenaran)* is never based on material wealth, power or force, but on qualities of spiritual qualities of greatness, for "the Javanese never hold the accumulation of material goods to be a person's aim in life". A clear statement yet one which was not hastily formulated, for we should realize the writer's scholarly environment at the time he wrote this passage.

As we have said, at that time Mr. Laksono was one of a small group of Indonesian graduates seconded to Leiden University. One of the main purposes of their research period in the Netherlands was to allow them to become familiar with the Dutch-language publications on the regions each of them was studying; in Mr. Laksono's case, the Bagelen region of Java. That is to say, he, like the other members of the group, had been studying publications on Indonesia as seen through Dutch eyes. At the same time (thanks to his training in Indonesia, his work in Leiden, and his own scholarly inclination) he was developing an affinity to the Leiden tradition of structural anthropology, the trend within our discipline which attaches prime importance to the cognitive approach, i.e. to ascertaining how the participants in a culture perceive and think about their own social and cultural environment. It is clear that the Indonesian graduates were thus in a position that they had to carry out two assignments, which might appear to be incompatible: to study foreign (viz. Dutch) analyses of the cultures of their specialization, while paying great attention to the views of the cultural participants – to whom, in most cases, they themselves belong (cp. P.E. de Josselin de Jong 1984). That Laksono, for one, did not shirk this task – "paradoxical" in every sense – will be apparent from the passage we are now discussing, and from several others in chapter III. Investigating the traditional structure by means of a model, he is acting as the observer from outside; dealing with the relative importance which "the Javanese" attach to material and spiritual qualities, he is speaking from within, as a participant[2].

Section II.4 further develops the study of the ruler's relation to his realm, which had been introduced in II.3. Earlier in this Foreword we had already seen that *tradition* is accentuated, but is not synonymous with static. Footnote 34 offers an excellent proof of this. It summarizes the contexts of the highly relevant myth of *Baron Sakèndhèr,* which explaints that the Dutch, apparently foreign intruders in Java, are actually of Javanese descent. That is to say, the myth converts change into an aspect of tradition.

The discussion then gradually concentrates on Javanese kingship from the 18th century onwards, until it reaches its climax

---

2) I do not think I am betraying a confidence when I add that, in discussing an earlier draft of chapter II with him, I asked whether he was justified in saying that *"the* Javanese" hold certain opinions. His answer showed how clearly he realized his paradoxical situation, and also how courageously he faced it: "I am a Javanese, and all my aquaintances and I hold this opinion; so it is a fact that this opinion is held in Java. How widely it is held is a matter for a later investigation."

in the figure of Prince Diponegoro. Diponegoro, for whom Arjuna was probably the ideal; who acts as *mediator* by using both his Javanese and his Arabic name; who is *initiated* by his sharing of the common people's trials and sorrows, and by his pilgrimage to Sultan Agung's grave.

This section is so rich in its contents, setting the Java War, and Diponegoro in particular, into the context of Javanese tradition, that it may seem pretentious to appeal to the active reader to proceed further along the path which Laksono so clearly defines. Yet, here again, a book expressly limited to Java contributes to our knowledge of Indonesia as a FAS. I need only mention the themes of the ruler as mediator and the ruler as initiate, which we also discern in Sumatran literatures; in addition, the theme of the Old and the New Dynasty interacting. When Diponegoro hears Nyai Rara Kidul speak to him, he understands that she is foretelling the battles which will precede a new dynasty; and Diponegoro's ideal, Arjuna, was also the ideal for Erlangga, who founded a new royal line (Berg 1938). At the same time, Diponegoro's pilgrimage to Imogiri was to venerate Sultan Agung as one of the ancestors of the old line of the house of Mataram, to which Diponegoro also belongs.

When we called Diponegoro a mediator, this was because the author so convincingly brings out this feature of his life and his deeds. Chapter II could have no better ending than the four-cell model, by which Diponegoro's position in the ambivalent and total central point is demonstrated.

Chapter III is devoted to Bagelen, the author's home district, so it is not surprising that his personal knowledge plays a part in his account. It would be a mistake, however, to suppose that this chapter will prove to be very inward-looking. As we observed before, the various features we distinguish in the book as a whole are interwoven. Thus in chapter III, the small world of Bagelen is not so dominant that the great world of Indonesia as a FAS retires to the background. We have an example of the first aspect in section III.1, where the author quotes from his conversation with a Javanese who (as a true structuralist, although he will not be aware of the fact) theorizes that the differences between the days of the week are in accordance with *(cocok dengan)* differences between people's characters. This is in complete agreement with one of the more famous pronouncements of Lévi-Strauss (1962: 111): "It is the differences which resemble each other"! In the same section, however, Laksono returns to the ruler's position as the central figure, both figuratively and literally. Both his Javanese informant, speculating about the days of the week, and the author himself, carrying through his study of the ruler, are talking about classifications; but the former exemplifies a conversation at the local level, while the second is dealing with a topic one encounters throughout the FAS.

Section III.1 is, in fact, remarkable because it is particularly rich in material for two basic features of the book: the notion of *structure* and the use of the *model*. On the first, I need only mention one more instance beside the one we have just discussed, viz. the important footnote 7. In the classification systems, i.e. the structure, of Mataram one finds many binary oppositions, such as right-left, inside-outside, east-west, but hardly ever the north-south opposition. For all its apparent simplicity this is structural reasoning at its best. The researcher is not, as critics so often aver, merely building up opposition systems by his own ingenuity; no, by a critical attention to the empirical data he sees what is *not,* or apparently not given in the struture. This, in its turn, leads him to enquire whether the missing element may perhaps be found elsewhere; in this case, in mythology.

As regards the model, we refer to Table I, where Laksono develops his informant's idea into a "Table of Correspondences" based on the days of the Javanese five-day week. Here I think it may be useful to refer to a study on "maximal correspondences" (Miyazaki 1979), which Laksono touches on in Appendix 3 but does not discuss at this point. Miyazaki wondered whether such correspondences are "maximal", in the sense of unchanging: is the day Legi *always* associated with the colour white, the cardinal point east, etc.? His conclusion is that this is not the case. Further research on this point is needed and, I believe, will be forthcoming.

In section III.2 we once more see a detailed study of local (Bagelen) phenomena involving matters of fundamental importance for our now familiar themes of tradition, structure, model, local knowledge and the FAS. We shall summarize this as briefly as possible.

Returning to a subject discussed in II.3, the author notes that members of the ruling élite often require material goods from their subordinates. In the model, this locates them in cell III, the immanent-existential. However, this is not in accordance with the concept of the unity of Master and Lord, so they will have to legitimize their superior status. They do so particularly by their family histories (which one is justified in calling family myths), which stress their traditional background by means of genealogies. Here we may insert a note that James Fox (1971), starting out from data he obtained in the island of roti, has stressed the importance of the genealogical history as a literary *genre*, in Roti and (else-where). Once more, Laksono's Bagelen data illuminate research in the context of the FAS.

An additional note is that one more common criticism of structural anthropology is refuted in this section, namely, that this type of research is always "abstract", as it has no relevance for practical affairs. Now let us turn to a specimen of a genealogical myth discussed by Laksono: the *Salasilah ing Para Leluhur ing Kadanurejan*. It contains the episode where the hermit utters this prophecy to Bagus Janah: he will become a revered "founding father" *(cakal-bakal)*, and his descendants will become prominent leaders. The condition for the fulfillment of this prophecy is that he himself must undergo hardships (which, we may add, will serve to initiate him, as they did in the case of Prince Diponegoro). Actions for a *practical* aim are *structurally* interpreted in this (pas-sage).

The section continues, combining the model ("abstract, theoretical"?) with intimate knowledge ("empirical, practical"). As for landownership, a Javanese village is stratified, but we must always be aware of tendencies and countertendencies. It is stratified, but solidarity is also always manifested. Javanese thought does not stress the differences in status, wealth and power, but stresses what is common to all (for example, the villagers' common responsibility towards visitors). It moves in the model from cell III to IV, to what is existential and *transcendent*. This central thesis of Laksono's is the result of a fusion between his theoretical model and his intimate knowledge of life and thought in Bagelen.

The argument of section III.2, and in effect of the whole book, is that the Javanese are well *aware* of difference in social status and wealth, but proceed *beyond* this empirical registration of facts. Their true model is the unity of Servant and Lord. It is *their* model, Laksono is saying, and not an outside observer's construction. He can say this because he is not an outside observer.

In this excessively long Foreword I have tried to demonstrate how consistently the author, writing for actively co-operative readers, has interwoven six basic features which I shall enumerate for the very last time: tradition, structure and model; intimate knowledge of the observer from within; the central role of the ruler, exemplified above all by Prince Diponegoro; and contributions to our understanding of Indonesia as a Field of Anthropological Study.

The author's own summary and conclusions are given in chapter IV, which is so clear that I do not wish to spoil it by any comments of my own.

P.E. DE JOSSELIN DE JONG
Leiden University.

REFERENCE

Berg, C.C. 1938. De Arjuna Wiwaha, Erlangga's levensloop en bruiloftslied? *BKI* 93: 19—93.

Brown, C.C. 1952 Sejarah Melayu or "Malay Annals": a Translation of Raffles MS 18. *JMBRAS* 25: 1—276.

Dumont, Louis. 1970. *Homo Hierarchicus: the Caste System and its Implications.* Chicago: University of Chicago Press.

Fox, James J. 1971. A Rotinese Dynastic Genealogy: Structure and Event. In. T.O. Beidelman (ed.), *The Translation of Culture.* London: Tavistock; 39—77.

Jordaan, R.E. and P.E. de Josselin de Jong (forthcoming). The Sick King as a Metaphor in Indonesian Political Myths (to be published in) *BKI.*

Josselin de Jong, J.P.B. de. 1983. The Malay Archipelago as a Field of Ethnological *Study. In: P.E. de Josselin de Jong (ed.), Structural Anthroploogy in the Netherlands,* 2d edition. Foris Publications for Translation Series, Koninklijk Instituut voor Taal–, Land– en Volkenkunde 17: 166-182. (Originally published in Dutch in 1935).

Josselin de Jong, P.E. de. 1980 *Ruler and Realm: Political Myths in Western Indonesia.* Amsterdam: Mededelingen der Koninklijke Nederlandse Akademie van Wetenschappen, Afd. Letterkunde, Nieuwe Reeks 43–1.

——————————, 1984. *Waarnemer en waargenomene: wie is wie?* Leiden: Rijksuniversiteit te Leiden.

Lévi-Strauss, Claude. 1953. Social Structure. In: A.L. Kroeber (ed.), *Anthropology Today.* Chicago: University of Chicago Press: 524-553.

——————, 1962. *Le Totémisme Aujourd'hui*. Paris: Presses Univer-
sitaires de France.

Miyazaki, Koji. 1979. *The Problem of "Maximal Correspondence"*.
Leiden: ICA Publications no. 35.

Moyer, David Spencer. 1975. *The Logic of the Laws: a Structural Analy-
sis of Malay Language Legal Codes from Bengkulu*. The Hague:
Martinus Nijhoff for Verhandelingen, Koninklijk Instituut vor
Taal–, Land–, en Volkenkunde 75.

ABBREVIATIONS

BKI   *Bijdragen tot de Taal–, Land– en Volkenkunde* (Publis-
           hed by) Koninklijk Instituut voor Taal–, Land– en
           Volkenkunde.

ICA   Institute of Cultural Anthropology, Leiden University.

JMBRAS   *Journal of the Malayan Branch, Royal Asiatic Society*.

PREFACE

This small book represents part of the work done while I was a graduate student in the Anthropology Department at the University of Indonesia, and Leiden University. As I think back on all the problems encountered during its writing, I do not believe I could ever have brought it to completion without God's help.When I first began to collect the data for my research, I felt as if I had entered a spacious orchard bursting with ripe fruit. So many valuable contributions have been made to the vast body of existing literature on the subject of Javanese society that I hardly knew where to begin. The days slipped into weeks, and the weeks into months, and there I was, still spell-bound by the work of each social scientist who had left something of himself in the orchard of studies on Javanese society.

Finally, I decided to fashion this book into a garland of fruits and flowers plucked from those whose ideas I so deeply respect, and to add a little information gleaned from material in archives. To the reader I offer a caveat: no new facts are presented in this work. All I have done is to repeat and modify the analysis of others.

I have tried to formulate an explanation of a classical problem through a reinterpretation of existing data. One reason for selecting this type of approach is that very little time was allotted for doing research ; I began in January of 1983 and was supposed to have finished in May of the same year. As it turned out, it took so long to locate, read, understand, and rework the bulk of library and archival material that the final draft of this manuscript was not ready until March 1984.

There are still many shortcomings in this work as it stands now; they are due to lacunae in my knowledge of the society in which I, myself, am a participant. Therefore, I would welcome any criticism and suggestions which will help me to make the improvements I know must be made.

ACKNOWLEDGEMENTS

I am especially grateful to Professor Dr. Koentjaraningrat and Professor Dr. P. E. de Josselin de Jong for the valuable advice and guidance given to me throughout all stages of this book. I would also like to thank Dra. Anke Niehoff for organizing my studies during my stay in Holland, and Dr. C. Baks, who provided so much help with the sections on Indic culture.

I am deeply indebted to the Government of Indonesia and the Netherlands Government, both of which so generously provided financial assistance through the Dutch-Indonesian Joint Steering Committee for the Development of Indonesian Studies in Jakarta, and the Bureau Indonesische Studien in Leiden.

I also owe a tremendous debt to the authors on whose work I have drawn so heavily, and regret that there is no way to express my appreciation other than to write their names in my footnotes and bibliography. I would also like to thank all the library staff at the Koninklijk Instuut vor Taal Land-,en Volkenkunde in Leiden, especially Rini for never losing patience with me in the reference room.

My acknowledgements would not be complete without mentioning those who provided so much assistance of a non-formal nature. I am grateful to the Indonesian students at Leiden for their help in tracking down references, and for suggestions and criticism offered during seminars and in discussions over tea at the local automat. I would like to thank my sparring partners, Raymond Burhan and Father Kuntara Wiryamartana SJ, for personal encouragement and stimulation.

There are many others who gave me moral support during my graduate work. My special thanks to Dr. and Mrs. Teeuw and their family in Leiden, and to the J. Kastowo and A. Y. Suyitno family in Indonesia for always being there when I needed them. And finally, I would like to express my gratitude to my brother, Th. M. Priyanggiatno, and his family for all the loving care given to my daughter, Monica Maria Widi Setyorini.

P. M. Laksono

Yogyakarta 1984

CONTENTS

CONTENTS

I. CONCEPTUAL FRAMEWORK

It is interesting to speculate on what would have happened had Javanese social structure continued to move along the course it had been following prior to the nineteenth century and the imposition of direct colonial rule. This particular century is important because it was at this point that Western socio-cultural elements, which had hitherto remained on the periphery, began to penetrate the basic configuration of Javanese society and deflect it from its pre-colonial trajectory. The precise nature of this configuration and the magnitude of displacement caused by the Dutch has been the subject of much interest among Indonesian and non-Indonesia social scientist alike.

J.H. Boeke (1910) examined Dutch influence from the point of view of economics and came up with the well-known theory of economic dualism. Colonial penetration into Java was but a static expansion: oxidental (Dutch) economic expansion developed and prospered without absorbing the economy of the orient (Java), which was making no headway at all, since any financial gain accrued to the Javanese was soon negated by massive population growth. In analysing the meeting of East and West, Boeke employed two completely different standards of measurement, one of social relationships for Java, and one of capitalist economics for Holland. Boeke's theory purported that since Java was based on a homo-social mentality and Holland on one of homo-economics, the economies of both were different. Not surprisingly, his methodology was called into question, and the concept of economic dualism lost credence.[1]

Another group of analysts, among whom Van Vollenhoven figured notably, were mainly experts in *adat* (traditional) jurisprudence. They divided the nineteenth century into two periods, pre-colonial and colonial, in an effort to discover the form of 'traditional Javanese society', by which they meant society as it had existed prior to being subjected to Dutch influence. Primarily concerned with justifying the pre-eminent national goal of their times, ie, the communalization of land, they portrayed the village as a harmonic territorial and administrative unit, and completely disregarded social organization and stratification (Onghokham 1975:212).

This same view of an undifferentiated society is again reflected in D. H. Burger's work (1939: 4) on the advance of Dutch government and economy into Java.[2] Burger sliced the organization of Javanese society into four domains: that of the king, *bupati* (regent), village administrator, and peasantry. He then proceeded to demonstrate how the Dutch had penetrated at the top level of the king early in the seventeenth century and that of the regent late in the eighteenth. With the spread of the Cultivation System, Dutch influence reached into the domain of the village administrator and, by the end of the nineteenth century, had finally breached the wall of the peasantry (Burger 1975: 144). Burger's explanation was based around two concepts: *dorpsgenbondenheid*, horizontally equal latencies among villagers and vertical obli-

---

1. See for example A.M. Sievers (1974: 279–290) and Dewey (1962: 185–189). C. Geertz (1963: 142) attributes this difference not to an Eastern mentality, but rather to the emergence of a more dominant, modern industrial economy. B. White (1971 and 1983: 15) goes so far as to say that Javanese economy was integrated with, not autonomous of, that of the Dutch.
2. Geertz (1963: 82) would appear to be of the same opinion, because he regards the sharing of poverty as an undifferentiated factor of agricultural involution.

gations of obedience to village administrators; and *foedale gebondenheid*, the chain of command and obedience stemming from the king, regent and *priyayi* imposed upon the village from above (1939: 4–5). It was due to this final thrust of colonial authority into the peasantry that the village became monetized, with rural society undergoing changes which released individuals from a legacy of hereditary social ties (1975: 130).

Studies of more recent origin (Elson 1978; Kano 1980; White 1983) have attempted to show that Javanese society was not an undifferentiated mass and would therefore have been capable of responding in any number of different ways to external stimuli, such as the Cultivation System. The implications of such observations are clearly at odds with those arising from the view that nowhere in Javanese society was there any differentiation to be found. So, while Geertz (1963) may have thought that the Javanese responded to the Cultivation System by sharing their poverty, later analysts (for instance Elson 1978: 28) point out that it was this system itself which created a class of large landowners drawn from the upper strata of rural society. This is quite conceivable, as this group had wide organizational and supervisory powers in the system of forced deliveries and contingents. However, in order to fully understand the progression of colonialism through such venues as the Cultivation System, it will first be necessary to have more information on the three types of relationships involving peasant labour: work done for other villagers, for the plantation, and for the state (Onghokham 1975: 213).

There is a great range of differences in the studies of Javanese society-Dutch colonialism mentioned thus far, and yet through all there runs a common thread, this being the bearing which these scientists' perception of pre-colonial society had on the further development of their respective analyses. Because the nature of pre-colonial society is of such importance, what I have done in this work is to examine social structure in a region known socio-culturally as the *kejawen*. The first part of my analysis deals with certain facets of the larger dimension of the kingdom, and

4

the second with their transformation within the smaller dimension of the village as it existed in the former residency of Bagelen.

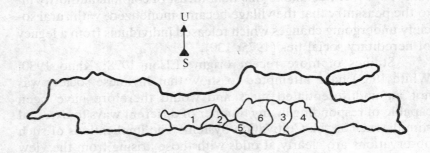

1. Banyumas
2. Bagelen
3. Madiun
4. Kediri
5. Yogyakarta
6. Surakarta

Source: Hogenholtz (1983: 6)

Map 1. Composition of the *Kejawen* (1–6)

The *kejawen* is that region which, until the end of the Diponegoro War, was still governed directly by the kingdoms of Surakarta and Yogyakarta, including Mangkunegaran and Pakualaman (ENI: 626). As the *kejawen* was isolated from direct contact with Dutch influence until 1830[3], it can be assumed that the region was a stronghold of undiluted and sophisticated Javanese tradition.

The exact geographic limits of the *kejawen* are difficult to ascertain, and this has led to a discrepancy between Geertz (1963:42) and Kano (1980: 5–6) as regards the location of the eastern border. Kano sets this border at Jombang, a good distance

3. This year has often been seen as a turning point, as *"a time when Javanese tradition turned in on itself and lost something of its strength and flexibility"* (Pigeaud 1967: 104–105).

west of Pasuruan, whereas Geertz places it much further east, running straight through Pasuruan. However, as there is no dispute over the position of Bagelen, which lies clearly within the *kejawen,* we need not concern ourselves any further at this point with boundaries. In actual fact, my interest in the *kejawen* is confined to that part of Mataram located in the *negaragung,* or core area of the kingdom, and randomly partitioned into two states, the sunanate of Surakarta and sultanate of Yogyakarta, in 1755 under the Treaty of Gianti. The territories of both states, particularly those in the *negaragung* became so interspersed that it is virtually impossible to tell where the jurisdiction of one left off and the other began. This is also true of Bagelen, where territories administered by Surakarta were mixed indiscriminately with those of Yogyakarta.

The reason that Bagelen, and not some other district, is featured in this work is that I had originally intended to include a discussion of spacial mobility, a phenomenon long peculiar to the area. As early as 1890 Heyting, a former resident, had transported large sections of Bagelen's population to Priangan as part of an experimental colonization initiative (ARA 6488: 507). However, as there was insufficient time to fully explore this area of inquiry, Bagelen is used here to illustrate certain aspects of tradition in rural society. Throughout this discourse, tradition has been treated as a hereditary choice exercised by the Javanese as a means of coming to terms with the basic facts of their existence, an existence which, as I see it, was inexorably bound up with the kingdom.This being the case, my analysis focuses on those features of the kingship tradition which, by means of a transformational model, can be shown to have reappeared within the dimension of the village.

I have analysed tradition within a framework of social structure and, as a dynamic of this structure itself. Since this is not a standard approach, it might be wise to say a few words at this point about the methodological orientation of this work. Lévi-Strauss (1963: 279) holds that social structure, being related with the formulation of *a posteriori* models, has nothing to do with empirical reality, and I can see no cause for argument with this. Social structure can under no circumstances be reduced to a set of social relations described in any one society, although the raw material for organizing social structure is contained within these social relations. Lévi-Strauss says that for a model to have structural value, it must meet four conditions: a) it must exhibit systemic features; if one component changes, all others must follow suit; b) it must lend itself to transformation [4] into other models of the same type; c) the conditions in (a) and (b) must enable one to predict how the model will react if one of its components changes; and d) it must explain all observable facts.

The details of this approach to social structure have been worked out by Pouwer, who describes structure as an elaboration of the mental process involved in communication, and thus related to the basic features of a semiotic system[5]. Pouwer has developed a number of principles which serve to position each component relative to another, thereby both constituting the system of relations known as structure and giving content to its form. These he classifies as: 1) fundamental structuring principles, 2) derived general structuring principles, and 3) derived particular structuring principles (1974: 241–242) [6].

---

4 What is meant here by transformation is the method of translating one system of semiotics into that of another (Rossi 1974: 89). In linguistics a transformation may be worked through in one of two ways: paradigmatically (a metaphor based on certain similarities) which is non-linear, and syntagmatically (a metonyme based on attributive analogy) which is linear. Paradigmatic-syntagmatic analysis was developed by de Saussure and the metaphoric-metonymic refinement added later by R. Jacobson (P. Ricoeur 1978: 230–233). Analysis of this type can be found in B. J. Macklin and N. R. Crumrine (1974).

5 See also P. Ricoeur (1978: 240–241).

6 A number of the examples supplied here to explain Pouwer's priciples are my own.

Fundamental structuring principles are of two types: identical positioning principles and contra-positioning principles. The first principle states that the position of some components, for example. king and commoner. becomes identical when placed in opposition to the position of another component. such as *Gusti**. The second principle states that the position of one or more components relative to that of others is different. as for example the position of priest and knight *(satria)* within the context of the kingdom.

There are three types of derived general structuring principles: reciprocal positioning, equi-positioning and supra-positioning. According to the first, positions arising from the principles of identical positioning and contra-positioning are interchangeable and hence the ostensible contradiction between likes and non-likes can be reconciled. Thus, it may be said that while knight and priest were dissimilar in terms of function, they evinced a similarity of needs, with the priest dependent upon the secular power of the knight and he, in turn, dependent upon the sacral authority of the priest. The reciprocal nature of their relationship does not deny their differences, but states that these differences can be integrated because of mutuality of need [7]. The second principle, equi-positioning, states that the position of some components relative to that of others is on the same level, as

---

* The word *Gusti*, meaning lord, is one of those nebulous Javanese terms which, depending on the context, can have either the mystical-religious connotation of Superior Being-God, or the secular connotation of king-authority figure. The implications of this double connotation will become apparent in later sections of the book (translator's note).

7 The principles of equivalence, opposition and reciprocality occur in Lévi-Strauss' description of kinship as a dialectic framework between the principle of correlation, as an inner-group set of relationships, and the principle of opposition, as inter–group opposition. The principle of reciprocality is viewed as a synthesis appearing as incest prohibitions, dual organizations and cross-cousin marriage (Rossi 1974: 111).

8

for example, in the case of peer relationships. According to the third principle, there is a disparity in the position of some components relative to that of another, as is seen in the commoners' position relative to the King's in terms of authority.

Derived particular structuring principles are also of three types. The first, vertical positioning, can be seen operating at the level of rules determining lineal descent. The second, horizontal positioning, is manifested in Hawaiian-type kinship systems, which are based on generation-sets. Finally, there is concentric positioning, which is found in kindred-oriented systems differentiating between near and distant kin on the basis of ever-widening circles of relationships.

To make an analysis of structural significance requires that the number of priciples involved be limited. This will enable one to learn the relative positions and weights of certain principles within a given configuration, since not all principles will operate at the same weight in the object of study. In this way, a given structural configuration can be classified and then compared with other configurations. Thus the comparison will mainly deal with the relative positions and weights of those principles from another configuration which are relevant. This step of analysis requires models, and Pouwer (1974: 243) provides further elucidation of what is meant by a model [8]. A model is an explicitly formulated metaphor containing a number of mutually dependent components and, as such, cannot be regarded as part of the data it represents, the rationale being that every model is required to describe something larger or different from the data. Such a description can be effected by presenting the data in the form of: (a) a summary (type, diagram), (b) a correlation (pattern), (c) an idealization (paradigm or ideal-type), (d) a configuration (gestalt, style or structure,

---

8. The concept of models in structuralism has often been misconstrued. For a discussion of this, see A. de Ruijter (1977 : 211–220) and Nutini (in Hayes 1970 : 70 –108).

and (e) any combination of these four. Thus, Pouwer considers a model to be a compact metaphor useful for comparing selected data and selected components within a logical configuration (1974: 243).

Having run briefly through the concept of structure, and its relating concepts, it is now time to clarify the notion of tradition. When tradition [9] is taken as a dynamic of particular society, it can be interpreted either diachronically or synchronically. The problem with a diachronic approach is that it leads to a disjointed understanding of tradition as a continuum of values from the past at logger heads with modernity, which is of course full of change. A diachronic approach also raises the question of how far tradition is related to an unchanging past – which does in fact change – and how far a normative representation of the past can be consistently applied as a standard for the continuation of change from a situation in the present (Locher 1978: 170). The second question is intended as an indication of the need to develop a synchronic approach to tradition. I agree with C. J. Heesterman (1985: 10–11) who sees tradition in terms of its meaning and function. Tradition represents a way for society to formulate and deal with the basic facts of human existence and, as such, is a consensus reached by society on life and death matters, including the problem of eating and drinking. In this respect tradition is not different from modernity. Since there is never any final solution to these basic problems, if tradition is to survive over time it must be flexible and fluid, situational rather than absolute. Not only does tradition have to be flexible and fluid, but because its primary task is to deal in a structured way with life and death problems, which cannot be solved, it must also present a plant or order

---

9. It should be noted that the idea of continuum is embedded in the origin of the word tradition, ie, from *tradere*, meaning to hand down.

which is above and beyond the actual situation. Tradition must, then, provide the transcendent order which becomes the basic orientation for legitimating human actions. However, tradition must be immanent in the actual situation so as to conform with shifts in reality at the same time as it is transcendent in order to fulfil its orienting and legitimating function[10]. It is this dual function which brings us to the crux of tradition: its inherent inner-conflict. Tradition is determined by a specific form reflecting the conflict between its immanence in society and its transcendent aspirations concerning the basic problems of human existence. If anywhere there is a key to understanding the dynamic element in the structure of a society organized by inner-conflict, then surely it must be here. The dynamics of such a society should be explainable by means of a model and, to get just the right sort of model, I have tried to be attentive to analysis done at the statistical, normative, and cognitive levels. At the first level, particular notice has been taken of genuine events whose frequency can be used to establish a pattern. At the second level, explicit and implicit norms and values, which stimulate as well as control the behavior of participants in the society and culture under observation, are noted. Lastly, attention has been given to the participants' categorization of the phenomena with which they are confronted (Pouwer 1974: 244)[11].

---

10. Cf. Spradley and McCurdy (1980 : 7).
11. A. de Ruijter (1981 : 194) compares these three levels of analysis with the three types of participant views distinguished by P. E. de Josselin de Jong (1977).

II. JAVANESE KINGSHIP

1. Approaches to the Kingship Tradition

The contributions of B. Schrieke and Soemarsaid Moertono to the study of Javanese kingship, particularly that of the second Mataram kingdom, are such that one would be hard pressed to discuss this subject without making reference to their work. In fact, one work is really an extension of the other. Moertono (1981: 1) based his analysis on research cut short by Schrieke's death[1], and supplemented it with de Graff's review of Mataram history[2] and Javanese manuscripts: *piwulang* (books of ethical instruction) and *babad* (chronicles), in an effort to bring the original concept to its logical conclusion.

The best place to begin is probably with a discussion of the two central issues identified by Moertono in the kingship of Mataram, ie, the king's authority, and the technical and material implementation of this authority. In his exploration of the means by which the king legitimated his hegemony over all others in the kingdom, Moertono draws our attention to the importance of magico–religious concepts in implementing royal authority and in maintaining the integrity of the state, concepts which played no small role in a kingdom so sacrosanct in character as Mataram. State organization was based on the need to preserve a certain

---

1. This refers to *Indonesian Sociological Studies,* esp. Vol. II (1957).
2. This refers mainly to *Geschiedenis van Indonesie* (1949).

order inspired by macrocosmic regularity and manifested in the harmonic flow of natural phenomena. In order to empathize with this larger order, the Javanese first had to accept the idea of harmonic order as a *sine qua non* not restricted only to the synchromesh of the macrocosmos and microcosmos (tangible world of the senses) but also encompassing the *batin*, the inner realm of spiritual, emotional and intellectual life. The intricate balance of these three harmonies is neatly summed up by the Javanese expression *tatatentrem**. One way of creating this triad of harmonies was through religious practices: the structures and institutions involved in the worship of the gods with all their rules and rituals, including all the ceremonial paraphernalia required for this purpose (Moertono 1981: 3). Such activities represented an effort on the part of man to establish a bridge between his own world and that of the gods. In this way, an attempt was made to devise a means of protecting the harmony of the natural enviroment against possible disturbances from the social (microcosmic) and macrocosmic order, all three of which were held to be interdependent. On the basis of these concepts, Moertono defines the function of social organization (the kingdom) as being primarily concerned with the visible manifestations of harmony.

> "In this sense social organization is not involvement in the members' daily routine but in maintaining adherence to established social patterns, the main manifestation of harmony. So its agencies primarily enforce such adherence, guarding against possible deviations and erasing whatever damage has been done, by magico-religious means as well as penal measures of a physical character." (1981: 3)

Furthermore, in such an arrangement, the king was expected to uphold the established order and not to introduce any innovations (1981: 4).

---

*   This expression is used interchangeably with the words tri-harmonic order and cosmological order throughout the book (translator's note).

From the description of social organization just presented one could hardly be blamed for arriving at a normative view of Javanese kingship where, analytically, the idea of the king as an agent of change would be given too little emphasis. And yet if we look at what really occurred, we cannot but see that the king's role was much more complex; he was even thought capable of setting the whole system of political order to vibrating. Javanese history abounds with examples of just how important the king's position was in creating-destroying and unifying-fragmenting the kingdom[3]. To obtain an analysis of greater magnification, I have modified Moertono's approach, incorporating it within the wider scope of tradition so that the working out of kingship on both a magico-religious and technical-administrative plane may be placed completely within the entire context of the dynamics of Javanese society. If Moertono's approach is summerized in diagram form, it can be drawn as:

Implementation of Kingship	
magico-religious (theory)	thechnical-administrative (practice)

Figure 1. Soemarsaid Moertono's Approach to Javanese Kingship.

Then, if this diagram is joined with the concept of tradition, the distinctive feature of which is the paradox between transcendence and immanence, the concept of kingship can be re-drawn and will, for the time being, be represented as:

---

3. See M. C. Ricklefs (1973).

Tradition

Javanese Kingship	magico-religious (theory); transcendent	magico-religious (theory); immanent
	non-material, spiritual, transcendent practices	material, natural, immanent practices

Figure 2. The Javanese Kingship Tradition.

It should be noted that this model is only temporary as it will later be shown to be inadequate for explaining all the facts of Javanese kingship.

According to the transcendent side of the model, kingship must characterize something ethereal, as it were, and absolutely beyond reach of the five senses. In classical times this was conceptualized by associating it with the situation in the supernatural realm where the gods' role was absolute in guaranteeing the perpetuation of order in the macrocosmos. This transcendent model led human logic to regard the authority of the gods as the only true model of the universe and, by corollary, the one and only way of resolving life death issues. The gods, as the highest authority-figures, would then have occupied a supra-ordinate position, becoming the apogee in the cosmological hierarchy of order. The premise for formulating such a model is the principle of supra-positioning where, it will be remembered, one component (e.g. the gods) is absolute and higher than another component (e.g. human beings). Such a structuring principle would appear in a dichotomic classification system in which the idea of sacred or pure was diametrically opposed to that of profane or impure.

The extent to which supra-positioning was embodied in Javanese tradition is a matter for further investigation, particularly because this principle frequently results in a classification system of polar opposites leading to extreme dogmatism. Javanese tradition is, on the contrary, often regarded as having been full of tole-

15

ration (Anderson 1965), or as having exhibited the qualities of *momong* (nuturing), *momot* (taking up), and *memangkat* (yielding) (Mulyono 1978 a: 252). Such an investigation would, therefore, require the comparison of a system in which the sacred: profane classification had been consistently applied. I have used the Indic world view for comparative purposes here, and in later phases of this discussion, since it is in India that the basic opposition, pure: impure, is seen most clearly in operation (Dumont 1970).

In Hindu sections of Indic society the dichotomous classification, pure: impure, became the principle underlying the operation of the caste system [4] because it was the distinctive feature of a hierarchy capable of generating an infinite number of segmentations and of expressing social relations in the form of occupational separation and specialization (Dumont 1970:251) [5]. It was in this way that India came to be divided into a great number of castes

---

4. Hinduism differentiates between the concepts of caste and *varna*. Both terms are homologous but there is a vast difference between the two. There are, for example, a great many more castes than those found in the *varna* system. Whereas the number of cases is virtually uncountable, everywhere in India *varna* comprises only: Brahman (priestly and scholarly élite); Ksatriya (secular-military leaders); Waisya (tradesmen, artisans and farmers); and Sudra (menials and unskilled labourers) with one additional non-*varna* group, the Harijan (Untouchables). Moreover, in *varna* theory, kingship is not hereditary while in the caste system, it is. Srinivas (1966 : 8) sees castes as lineal endogamous groups comprising a hierarchy, with each group having a traditional link with one or two occupations.

5. There are two differences to note in the caste system: the scale of religious statuses, which Dumont calls the hierarchy, and the distribution of economic and political authority – very important in practice, but further down on the scale. The Brahman occupied the apex of the hierarchy, but economic and political power resided with the king. If the Brahman were spiritually and absolutely at the apex but materially dependent, the king was materially dominant but spiritually subordinate. A similar type of relationship existed between actions done for the betterment of cosmological order (*dharma*), and those done in the interests of the individual (*artha*), where *artha* was only legitimated within the confines of *dharma*. Clearly then, the chief function of the hierarchy, the scale of religious statuses, was the ordering of the cosmos (Dumont 1970 : 251).

marked, on the one hand, by prohobitions against inter-caste *cunnubium* and *convivium* and by occupational specialization, on the other. Although Java did go through a period of exposure to Indic influence, the caste system, as it appears in India, never took root. This fact is often explained by reference to the Javanese proclivity for filtering out certain elements of foreign culture upon their arrival. While this observation may be correct, it still does not explain why some elements should have been accepted and others rejected. As I see it, the reason the caste system never caught on in Java is that there were logical processes already at the work within indigenous society which were opposed to the system of thought giving rise to a caste configuration.

It may have happened that the caste system was able to survive and flourish in India because the principle of hierarchy was logically compatible with that of Hindu social relations: caste endogamy, or the rejection of inter-caste marriage and commensality. The connection between castes and social relations can be further explored along the line of inquiry pursued by Lévi-Strauss (1966: 109–131). The development of castes is explainable by means of models of relations found in both nature and culture. The natural model is apparent in the relationship between natural species, where one species is so differentiated from another that no cross-breeding may occur. A cultural model, on the other hand, describes something which is really homogeneous as being culturally heterogeneous. An approach of this type is based on the idea that exchanges of food and women are a means of guaranteeing or demonstrating interdependence between social groups. In the case of castes, groups which were actually exopractising, as far as exchanges of goods and services were concerned, proved to be endopractising when it came to marriage. Castes can be taken to constitute a social species and, as such, were able to transfer goods and services because these represented manufactured objects or operations performed by means of techniques and equipment, ie, social products culturally produced by technical agents. Women, however, are biological individuals, ie, natural products, naturally procreated by means of other biological individuals.

Thus, it was occupational specialization, as seen from inter-caste exchanges of goods and services, which provided the feature making each caste truly different and, hence, mutually complimentary. Exchanges of women were a different matter altogether. As far as nature is concerned, women are homogeneous and can only be regarded as otherwise from a cultural point of view. Castes assimilated models of natural species and designated that on a cultural plane women were to become a naturally heterogeneous species. Caste endogamy came about because women were acknowledged as being alike only within the confines of their own social group and consequently non-transferable from one caste to another. Castes extracted the greatest possible advantage from cultural heterogenity. Hence, the exchange of women within a single group became a question of the accumulation of "functions", since caste endogamy strengthened existing occuptional specialization.

The analysis summerized above is wholly concerned with a mental plane very closely related with Louis Dumont's examination of the aspects of a religious hierarchy. It is also possible to discern the logical complimentarity between the division of labour – although Lévi–Strauss does not make the link-up with the pure: impure classification system – and the principle of social relations exhibited by caste endogamy. This complimentarity was an integral part of the caste system as well as being transcendent, or beyond empirical reality ; it was, in short, one condition for the operation of the caste system.

It is unlikely that conditions such as those just described were present in classical Javanese society. On the basis of research into contemporary Javanese kinship systems (Koentjaraningrat 1957: 13), there is no evidence for assuming that Javanese society practised anything other than nuclear family exogamy without explicit preference[6], apart from the nobility and *kauman*[7]

---

6. Relatively speaking, preference in marriage partners is expressed in the words: *bibit, bebet, bobot,* meaning one who is sound mind and body, of good parentage and character.

7. *Kauman* is that area of *santri,* or orthodox Muslim, concentration in the vicinity of urban mosques.

groups, where endogamous preference has been fairly customary. Moreover, there have never been any cases of exclusively hereditary occupational specialization. It might even be said that Javanese society exhibits a praxis which goes against the very fibre of the principle of hierarchy: the *selamatan*.

One of the hallmarks of Javanese society, the *selamatan* is a familiar, unpretentious commensal ritual performed at such critical junctures in one's life as birth, circumcision, recovery from illness, and even admission to university. To explain the significance of the *selamatan* as an actualization of Javanese social relations suffice it to quote from an informant of C. Geertz:

> "When you're at a *selamatan*, nobody feels different from anybody else and so you don't want to be all split up." Geertz adds: "At a *selamatan* everyone is treated equally. Consequently no one feels lower than the others, no one would see the need for humbling himself before his fellows" (1983: 17).

These words are indicative of the gulf between the principle governing social relations among the Javanese, and in castes, the latter of which are frequently associated with the Hindu concept of religious hierarchy. Nonetheless, the principle embodied in the *selamatan* is also at variance with the phenomenun of social stratification, which does in fact exist, and is acknowledged by the Javanese themselves. I, personally, have observed that during a *selamatan* social differences do on occasion make their presence felt, as for example, when certain people considered important by the host are offered a china plate while other guests must make do with a banana-leaf plate. Or, if everyone is eating off plates, the best china and cutlery will be reserved for important guests. While this clearly shows the contradiction between principle and practice, it certainly does not conceal the conflict between Javanese and Indic logic where caste was concerned.

If one looks at the occurrence of paradoxical figures[8] in

---

8. In contemporary philosophy, this type of problem resembles the debate surrounding two-, three-, or multi-valued logic (see Rosser and Turquette 1978 : 320–326; and Putuam 1978 : 327–34).

Javanese mythology, it would not be unreasonable to suppose that they were used to come to terms with the conflict between indigenous and Indic principles. They may even have been devised prior to Indic contact as a method of dealing with the inner-conflict in Javanese tradition, and only later became the logical premise for accepting Hinduism while rejecting castes.[9] These paradoxical figures occupied a central position in *wayang* legends, many of which were taken from the *Mahabarata* and *Ramayana* epics.

It should by now be evident that classical Javanese society had a model of relations different from that of a caste society, the main difference being that Javanese social structure was not exclusively founded on the principles of supra- and contra-positioning. When this fact is related to the kingship tradition, it becomes necessary to again question the extent to which kingship resembled the hierarchical model of the gods, for there is no getting away from the fact that this hierarchy was based on the belief in their absolute authority.

2. Kingship in the Wayang Tradition

Without a discussion of the *wayang* it would be difficult to appreciate all the ramifications of kingship I intend to present from this point onwards. Because the *wayang* contains a vast store of concepts and models used by the Javanese to interpret their world, it is to this artistic tradition of shadow puppetry that I now turn for the next phase in my analysis of kingship.

It has been said that the *wayang* represented all efforts on the part of the Javanese to describe the universe and their place

9. In the Majapahit era, there is some evidence that the existence of *catur warna* (four *varna*) was acknowledged, but this is thought to be nothing more than a theoretical embellishment to court literature (Kartodirdjo 1969 : 16). Because of inter-class mobility, it was possible to overcome all barriers between ruler and ruled, secular and religious groups, and freemen and slaves.

within it, to explain their relationship with the natural and supernatural world, with their fellows, and with themselves (Anderson 1965: 5). The puppets in the *wayang* assemblage provided the symbols needed to fathom the inner-content and basic attributes of human nature; the *satria* in particular became the model after which kings, nobles and ministers fashioned their authority. There would probably be no other way of exploring the implications of this statement than to examine, *lakon* by *lakon*, the logical structure of what has been called a religious mythology almost universally accepted by the Javanese – a task which I am ill-equipped to undertake. In lieu of this, I propose to offer an *a postiori* projection, nothing more, of classical Javanese thought as conveyed through one or two *lakon* adapted from the *Mahabarata* epic.

In the *Mahabarata* version discussed here[10], the plot revolves around events taking place in the celestial kingdom of Astina. In the beginning, Astina was a prosperous kingdom ruled with wisdom and justice by Nahusa's son, Prabu Yayati. Yet it was this same Yayati who became the source of all altercation when, in a moment of amorous indiscretion with a palace attendant, he committed a grave offence against Dewayani, his senior consort. Had the King managed to conceal his misdeed, no one would have been the wiser, and the story would have been over before it had barely begun. Now it just so happened that Yayati was found 'in flagrante delicto' by Dewayani who thereupon screamed and cried, creating the sort of commotion one would expect her to under the circumstances. Naturally, she went straight to her father, Resi Sukra, with the tale of her husband's transgression. Her father, who was a very powerful priest, managed to stay his hand against the King, but his sense of justice was too outraged to remain still. From the depths of his being he conjured an

---

10. I have relied heavily on Mulyono for material used in the discussion of the *wayang;* excerpts from the *Mahabarata* are drawn almost exclusively from Mulyono (1977).

arcane oath: "Sire, my Sovereign Lord, by this henious deed, thou hast befouled thy person, thy position, and even thy youth." Scarcely has this incantation been uttered than the enchantment began to work and, within the space of a few short minutes, Prabu Yayati shriveled up and turned into an aged, decrepit monarch. The time-ravaged Yayati implored Resi Sukra to lift the enchantment, but this was beyond the priest's science: "Alas, my Liege, what has been done cannot be undone, unless there lives a mortal who wouldst sacrifice his youthful countenance for thy wizen visage."

From these few lines emerge the earliest logical structures of the *Mahabarata* epic. First there was equilibrium, ie, an idyllic kingdom under a benevolent ruler. Then transgression entered by way of sexual indulgence; punishment followed swiftly in the form a spell cast by sacerdotal individual of spotless character, ie, Resi Sukra, whose incantation served as a purificatory force. The incantation together with the idea of *titah* (fate, destiny) and *takdir* (divine will, predetermination) sought to purge the story of all wrongs, evil and pollution having occurred thus far. At this point, the situation is still within the context of religion, but has now moved to the immanent side of the kingship tradition model (Fig.2). However as the plot unfolds, it is as if this effort to isolate the negative elements in the story serves only to produce greater disorder This is borne out by the next instances of corporeal-material indulgence.

The wretched Prabu Yayati was by now awash in feelings of desperation and humiliation. Still hungering after sensual gratification, self-aggrandisement and power, he summoned his five sons, saying: "My children, I grow ill with yearning for all the glory, honour and might which are mine by right. I would that one among ye forfeit his youth that I may cast aside the burden of this suffering inflicted upon my august person ......" Only the King's youngest son could bring himself to submit to a command of such monstrous proportions: "My father, High-King Binatara! I, Puru, do gladly surrender my youth that thou may be restored in strength of body and tranquillity of heart to rule over Astina once more." Without further ado Prabu Yayati embrased the boy, regaining his youth at the expense of his own son's. He plunged back into a life of debauchery, spending his nights in gluttonous feasting and cavorting, and his days in ruthless pursuit of mammon.

While this scene provided ample demonstration of how concupiscence and material ambition evolved to form the basis of human behavior, the picture would not have been complete without a moral reminder of the price extracted for such blatent unrestraint. Prabu Yayati's lament to his son both explains and brings to a close that part of the story where licentiousness and materiality gain ascendancy:

> "Ah Puru ..... my beloved son. I tell thee now that a lust unleashed does not abate. Indulgence stokes the flame of desire; it quenches it not. Like a snowball, it grows larger at every turn. Since falling prey to my own passions, my heart has known no peace ...."

The message clearly reads that serenity of self was not to be attained by giving in to libidinous urges, but rather lay in the following course of action:

> "Henceforth, I shall lead a life of abstinence, ... for it is only by suppressing my passions that I shall subdue them. Puru, my son, that I may find my way back into Divine favour, take back thy youth. Rule our people with wisdom, justice and benevolence that they may ever pay homage to thy royal will."

So saying, Prabu Yayati again shouldered the burden of his accursed age and in so doing demonstrated that he had broken through the barrier of worldly desires, since by submitting to the inevitability of Resi Sukra's incantation, he had brought himself that much closer to inner purity. The scene ends with Puru being annointed High-King of Astina, entrusted with the task of restoring justice and harmony to the kingdom. Puru's descendents became the Pandawa and Korawa[11], the feuding factions in the

---

11. See Appendix 1 for a complete breakdown of the Pandawa–Korawa genealogy.

later battle for the throne of Astina. The victory of the Pandawa, the rightful heirs, in the Baratayuda (Great Throne War) would probably have been interpreted as a return to the original state of equilibrium in Astina.

The foregoing analysis sets out the basic structure on which the Mahabarata was constructed, this being the separation of two irreconcilable elements, purity and impurity, or the sacred and profane. Impurity-profanity could only be eliminated by such purificatory means as incantations, *titah* and *takdir*. This was effected by placing profane elements (evil or corporeal desires) in opposition to those representing purity, sacrality, and spirituality. It was only after release from all physical and material desires had occurred that purity could be restored. However, since efforts aimed at release from the bondage of these desires were in opposition to purificatory incantations and *takdir,* they also entailed the rejection of such devices and occurrences, or a return to the pure situation.

The fact that the *Mahabarata* was Javanized shows that the Javanese of classical times did not categorically accept the logical structure of the epic. *Mahabarata* rhetoric contained certain elements diametrically opposed to social relations and to Javanese social structure, which tended to favour the identical, reciprocal and equi-positioning of the various components making up the configuration of indigenous society. An ingenious solution to this conflict was accomplished by placing the figure of Semar and the other *punakawan* in the centre–most position of the Mahabarata model. The *punakawan* are thought to have originally been an anthropomorphous representations of the common man, the masses, identified in Javanese by the words, *rakyat* and *wong cilik* (lit. little people). But just as surely as they played comical servant to the lofty Pandawa and Korawa knights, they were also portrayed as the devoted followers and, at the same time, mentors of their lords. Indeed, these particular puppets were, and for that matter still are*, so vital to the content of the shadow performance that a

---

*   The *wayang* is a living tradition, and so much of the information presented here is still true today (translator's note).

wayang would simply not be a *wayang* without them (Moertono 1981: 12).

The *punakawan* assemblage comprises Semar and his three foster-sons: Gareng, Petruk and Bagong—featured on the right side of the screen-kingdom—and Togog and Bilung, who appear on the left. In *wayang* mythology, Semar and Togog were really gods sent down to earth to perform a special mission. They form two-thirds of a triad: Togog, the eldest, also known as Batara Antaga Semar or *(who was none other than the Javanese ancestral spirit)* Batara Ismaya, and Betara Manikmaya or Batara Guru (Shiva) who ruled the celestial kingdom of the gods and also went under the name Great Teacher. Semar was by far the most important and dynamic of the three; he and his foster-sons were a constant source of encouragement to the harried Pandawa and never failed to help them out of difficulties. The Semar-Pandawa relationship epitomized all that a perfect democracy should be: the harmonic unity of king and commoner, expressed in Javanese as: *jumbuhing kawula-Gusti*. Furthermore, the multi-paradoxical iconography of Semar affords us greater breadth of vision into the world of classical Javanese thought processes. Semar evokes the image of a swollen toad: his anterior and posterior surfaces are so equal in rotundity that it is impossible to tell whether he is standing or sitting; his face is a curious mix of obese androgynous features and feminine decoration. All of these taken in combination would certainly have made Semar the most arresting and well-recognised puppet in the whole cast of *wayang* characters. It seems pointless to further belabour this description when a simple quote from Sri Mulyono will so much better illustrate the unique place Semar held in the Javanese mind:

> "What manner of creation is this, who stands leaning on his* belly?
> *or is it, who sits rocking on his buttocks?*

---

*   The word *his* is not strictly accurate. Sri Mulyono uses the neuter *yi*, perhaps alluding to the fact that Semar is either a hermaphodite or a transvestite (translator).

The mid-day sun is sallow beside the radiance of his face.
How can such brilliance emanate from one as pallorous as a corpse?

No parents, no children has he. His smile misted in tears.
Bleak perils of humanity, softened in the gentle rain of his compassion.

Goodness itself, this god made man, who
Dominates the *satria* with servitude.

Kings grovel before him; gods honour him;
Even the Most-High does his bidding.

Invincible through non-deeds, omnipotence in inertia.
Here lies the source of his *sakti* (divine might).

Dawn at dusk, sunset at daybreak,
The perfect being: Ismaya."

(Mulyono 1978b : 166).

Figure 3. Semar

Since Semar was so paradoxical and so central to the *wayang,* it is hardly surprising that he should have become not only the focus of orientation in the classical Javanese mind[12] but also the feature distinguishing Javanese from Indic logic. His introduction modified the basic logical structure of the Mahabarata and Ramayana epics, the structural model of which was based on the classification of polar and disparate absolute oppossites, ie, pure: impure, or what Pouwer calls contra–and supra-positioning. In the Javanized version, the Indic model was transformed through the paradox of Semar into a multi-reciprocal model with no polar absolutes, in other words, a combination of identical, reciprocal and equi-positioning (Pouwer 1974). What is implied by the nature and position of the multi-paradoxical Semar neatly sums up the Javanese attitude to life:

> "Nothing is absolute, there are always twilights between night and day, grades between good and evil, shades between black and white, subtleties between love and hate, degrees between happiness and grief, as well as nuances between male and female." (Boediardjo 1978: 110).

At this juncture it seems advisable to use a diagram—albeit one 'constructed in retrospect'—showing a model of the structure underlying the statement on Javanese thought quoted above. As each quadrant of this model represents very different phenomena, I have prepared a sample analysis of the Javanese system of classification using the model below; the analysis is offered by way of clarification and appears in chart form on the following page. The structural model bears a certain resemblace to the kingship model (Fig.2) but a number of refinements have been added and diagrammed as:

---

12. On this point, I differ with Th. Pigeaud and W. H. Rassers who classify the Semar element as belonging to the set of which is opposed to that of 'youngs' (Pigeaud 1927 : 344–345). I have put more weight on Semar's central position, viz. the second of three brothers.

CHART I

SAMPLE ANALYSIS OF CLASSIFICATION SYSTEM USING THE MODEL OF JAVANESE LOGIC

Location in model	Relation in Classification superior	inferior	Notes
ES TR (quadrant I)	sacred pure extraphysical power Brahman * old commoner (wong cilik)	profane impure temporal power Kshatria young king (wong gede)	Essential purity in supraposition. Abstract, supernatural in character. Usually depicted through hierarchy of god-characters. Open to immanence, hence pollution may occur.
ES IM (quadrant II)	sacred pure extraphysical power Brahman old commoner	profane impure temporal power Kshatria young king	All processes such as divine will, fate, incantations, preventing and purging pollution due to supernatural immanence. Processes occur on essential or theoretical level
IM EX (quadrant III)	profane impure temporal power Kshatria young king	sacred pure extraphysical power Brahman old commoner	Existential worldliness in supraposition Emperical, natural and relatively changeable in character. Open to transcendence, hence purification may occur. Included here, are all emperical social relations. Due to this structure there may be social stratification based on control of material resources.
TR EX (quadrant IV)	profane impure temporal power Kshatria young king	sacred pure extraphysical power Brahman old commoner	Contains all purificatory practices aimed at severing attachment to material life. Actions are essential or visible. Due to release from immanent-existential influences, these actions are considered transcendental and often appear as conservatism.
(O-locus)	No classifications at O because multi-paradoxical relations defy definition. Javanese describe this locus in multi-paradoxic terms, such as are symbolized by Semar.		Focus of orientation and truest model for Javanese. All aspects of life are harmoniously united. None are superior or inferior. Inter-quadrant opposition is resolvable. No conflict between quadrants I and III or II and IV. This orientation held to be means of attaining *jumbuhing kawula-Gusti*, the ultimate reality and also the core of the Javanese belief: *suwung awang uwung*. Without this orientation there is only a structural model containing conflict with no synthesis, such as is found in the caste system.

* Pigeaud (1927:339–342) uses this opposition to analyse the *Serat Baron Sakendher*.

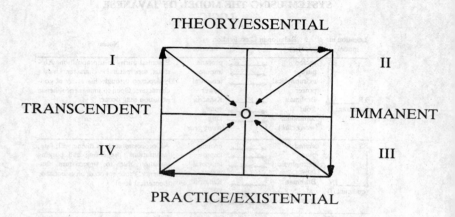

Figure 4. Model of Javanese Logic.

In quadrant I all phenomena which would have been classified as supernatural, spiritual and full of extraphysical power occupy a supra-ordinate position. In quadrant III the position is reversed, and all phenomena held to be natural, temporal, material, external, corporeal and authoritative occupy a supra-ordinate position. Quadrants II and IV contain phenomena which were thought to induce change. All supernaturally immanent processes bringing about change, ie, divine will, fate-destiny and incantations, appear ın quadrant II; all transendent human actions, ie, fasting, meditation (ascesis), aimed at withdrawal from the material world, and from the phenomena dominant in quadrant III, are found in quadrant IV.

This model attempts to portray the classical view of life by showing it as something moving from its transcendent-essential aspects in the direction of its immanent-existential aspects, passing through the essential-immanent, only to return to its transcendent-essential aspects by way of the transendent-essential. The clock-wise movement does not, however, fully reflect Javanese logic until diagonal lines are drawn to show the other principle affecting the course of human life, ie, the orientation towards the paradoxical centre. Sitting at the centre-most point was the figure of Semar, the archetype of the mystical consubstantiation of god and man and the secular unity of king and commoner, both of which concepts are expressed in the phrase: *jumbuhing kawula Gusti*. The centre point, or O-locus, also contained the core of the *Javanese belief system: suwung awang uwung*: the inexplicable calm and emptiness of the 'indeterminable' state attained wherein the (slices?) merged in perfect fusion with all aspects of life (transcendent, essential, immanent and existential)[13].

This may be somewhat pre-emptive, but I find this model very operational for getting at in integrated explanation of Javanese culture. Before moving into such a discussion, however, it will first be necessary to 'try out' the model by analysing the *lakon* found in *ruwatan*[14] of Sudamala.

---

13. In Javanese numerology all of these were characteristics of *das* or zero (Bratakesawa 1952 : 83–88).
14. *Ruwat :* delivered from the power of evil (incantations, misshapen creatures); 2. released from the bondage of nemisis. See Poerwodarminto (1939:543)

Exorcism–disenchantment *lakon* were closely aligned with Javanese ideas on the origin and purpose of life which began, not from an ideal image of humanity, but rather from human beings caught up in misfortune, enchanted by incantations, vulnerable to miscreation and deformities (Wiryamartana 1977 : 57–59).

The Structure of the Sudamala Lakon[15]

a. *The goddess Uma is cursed.* Sang Hyang Tunggal (the Unifier) and
Sang Hyang Wisesa (the Law Giver) go to Sang Hyang Batara Guru
(Great Teacher) to complain that Uma has betrayed her husband, ie,
Teacher himself.

This scene deals with events transpiring in the realm of the gods.
The gods' celestial abode is Kahyangan and these events would be
located in the transcendent-essential quadrant. Treachery of some
sort had occurred and the purity of Kahyangan has thus been vio-
lated.

Batara Guru becomes enraged and casts a spell changing the lovely goddess into Durga, a loathsome giantess. Teacher also foreordains that
Uma will be disenchanted by Sadewa, the youngest of the Pandawa brothers.

Here see we how the elements of incantation and fate were introduced. Uma was trasformed into Durga and has thus become immanent. In terms of the model, this would mean that life has begun to move towards its immanent-essential aspects.

Durga then descends to Setra Gandamayu (lit. place of stinking corpses)
and becomes leader of a coven of phantoms.

Further changes have brought Durga into collusion with spirits in
the ghoulish Setra Gandamayu. Durga was relegated to the lower
world and would then begin to enter the existential quadrant. Her

---

15. This *lakon* (one episode serving as the plot for a single night's *wayang* performance) tells of how Sadewa and Semar release a deity from enchantment. It is set within the context the dynastic dispute between the Pandawa and their kinsmen, the Korawa, and taken from an adaption made by
Sri Mulyono (1978b : 9–14).

place of residence may have been trascendent but she is still une-
quivically immanent because she was a giantess, which in *wayang*
rhetoric stands for a miscreation governed by passions and therefore in a constant state of disorderly turmoil.

b. *Citrasena is disciplined.* Two mischievous *gandarwa* fairies named Citrasena and Citrangganda spy on Batara Guru and his consort while
they are bathing in a lake. Teacher punishes their impudence by turning them into the giants. Kalantaka and Kalanjaya, and dispatching
them to the palace of King Duryudana where they are to be servants.

The themes in this scene parallel those in the previous one, and
would have served to create a mirror-image of nemisis, incantation, enchantment and entry into the world.

c. *Kunti becomes anxious.* The Pandawa brothers receive word that the
Korawa have enlisted the help of two very powerful giants. On hearing the news Kunti becomes frantic with worry over the safety of her
sons (the Pandawa). In this troubled state of mind, she slips quietly
away from the palace and goes to stay alone in Setra Gandamayu. Here
she meets Durga. When Kunti asks that the giants be got rid of,
Durga replies that it can be arranged provided that she is first present -
ed with a red sacrificial goat (metaphor for a Javanese). Kunti initial -
ly agrees but when she learns that what Durga has in in mind is actually her own son, Sadewa, she retracts and leaves.

The giants were used to create a disturbance in the balance of power between the Pandawa and Korawa, hence, this scene would
be in the existential-immanent quadrant. Emphasis also seems to
have been placed on Kunti's self-imposed isolation and probably
represented human efforts to leave the turbulent immanent quadrant and approach the transcendent, which is non-material and
therefore constant. At this point Kunti had not quite succeeded in
renouncing materiality since she could not yet hand her son over
to Durga.

d. *Kunti is possessed.* Soon after Kunti's exit, Durga commands the demon, Kalaka, to follow and take possession of her body. After this is accomplished, Kunti returns to the giantess in a state akin to madness and, no longer responsible for her actions, promises to return to the palace for her son.

The mother-child bond had to be severed in order to show that Kunti had truly relinquished all material ties. The fact that she was made to appear as having taken leave of her senses may well have been done to justify the totally irrational act of sacrificing one's own child to a Javanese audience, who would probably been unable to accept the symbolic import of this scene had it been presented in any other light.

e. *Sadewa becomes a sacrifical offering.* The Pandawa have been worried over their mother's unannounced departure and now rejoice at her home coming. But their happiness is short-lived, for Kunti soon reveals that Sadewa is to be given to Durga. If this is not done, a terrible misfortune will befall them all. Kunti takes Sadewa to Setra Gandamayu, gives him to Durga, and returns to the palace whereupon she falls into a deep sleep. The demon leaves her body and goes back to the lower world.

This scene shows that Kunti was finally free from all material–immanent concerns since she had given up Sadewa, her most prized possession. It is in this way that she reached the transcendent and was able to rid herself of the demon. Her sleep would seem to indicate that her earthly task had been completed.

f. *Semar waits with Sadewa.* In the meantime Sadewa has been tied to a tree and Semar is standing guard over him. The demon enters and offers to untie Sadewa if he will favour her with his attentions. After being released Sadewa refuses to comply with the demon's request. Infuriated, she summons forth a host of sordid creatures to torment the hapless Sadewa: centipedes, scorpions, all manner of ghouls and haunts. Sadewa remains unmoved. Durga then enters and begs him to release her from enchantment. Sadewa says that he cannot do this. He remains silent in the face of the giantess' threat to swallow him alive.

The Javanese would probably have interpreted Sadewa's stoic behavior as a sign of great mental concentration, ie, meditation, and this would put him in the transcendent quadrant. Through ascesis Sadewa was attempting to consummate the *kawula-Gusti* relationship, and thus bring himself to the O-locus of the model. He had not yet surmounted all barriers placed in his path because he was still struggling to resist the demon's temptations and Durga's pleas. It is interesting to note that throughout the whole scene the figure of Semar, the symbol of the goal Sadewa was trying to reach, hovers protectively in the background.

> g. *Mahendra informs Batara Guru.* Narada (the Wise) has been watching from afar and, realizing that unless something is done Sadewa will die before his time, asks Mahadewa for help. Mahadewa is reluctant to effect a rescue on his own, and so the two go to see Teacher.

Since Sadewa's plight was capable of stirring Narada and Mahadewa into action, this scene was probably intended to show the efficacy of meditation in bringing about a closer relationship between man and the gods. In terms of the model this type of relationship would come about in the existential-transcendent and transcendent-essential quadrants.

> h. *Sadewa disenchants Durga.* Batara Guru descends to Setra Gandamayu and commands Sadewa to bring Durga out of enchantment once he has entered his body. With Teacher now inside himself, Sadewa speaks: "I would that thee stand erect". Durga does as she is bid, her hideous form vanishes and her former beauty is restored.

With this scene we have finally arrived at the core of the Sudamala *lakon:* Durga's deliverance from the power of evil and release from the bondage of nemisis. Here was to be found the ultimate truth, that which was mighty enough to revoke fate: *manungga-ling kawula-Gusti,* the consubstantiation of god and man. This idea was conveyed through Sadewa (man) whose oneness with Batara Guru (god) overcame Durga (evil). It was probably not mere coincidence that the individual chosen to break Durga's enchantment had been given the name Sadewa. This name is formed from the prefix *sa:* one, and stem *dewa:* god. The consubstantiation of Sadewa and Batara Guru, being not only transcendent and existential but also essential and immanent, could not occur at any point in the model other than the O-locus.

i. *Sadewa is re-named.* The enchantment on Setra Gandamayu is now lifting, too. The brambles and vines roll back and all is lush and green once more; the demons and phantoms turn back into deities. As a token of her gratitude, the goddess Uma (alias Durga) bestows a new name, Sudamala (the Purifier), on Sadewa, and foreordains that he will marry Padapa, the daughter of the sage, Tambrapetra, at the Prang-Alas hermitage. She then flies back to her celestial home in Kahyangan.

This scene serves to explain the purpose of the *kawula-Gusti* consubstantiation, or the O-locus, this being the purifications of profanity, (i.e.), release form the power of evil forces. This was expressed in the meaning of Sadewa's new name and in the consummation of the divine-human relationship through the Purifier's marriage to the mortal, but pure, Padapa.

j. *Sadewa's marriage.* Semar accompanies Sadewa to the hermitage where he is duly married to the sage's daughter. Not to be outdone by his master, Semar waxes farcical and proposes to Towok, Padapa's lady-in-waiting.

    Then Raden Sakula (Nakula) goes to Setra Gandamayu in search of his twin-brother, Sadewa, Setra Gandamayu is now a verdent garden under the care of (the demon) Kalika. At first Kalika mistakes Sakula for his brother, but the mix-up is soon sorted out and Kalika directs

him to the hermitage. The brothers are re-united and Nakula marries
Soka, Padapa's sister.

In the reiteration of the *kawula-Gusti* theme, a multiple-image effect was created, thus extending the unity relationship at O in the
following way:

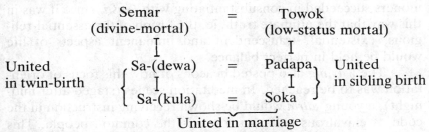

Figure 5. Extension of *Kawula-Gusti* Relationship.

k. *Sadewa disenchants Citrasena*. Meanwhile the giants, Kalantaka and
Kalanjaya, have attacked the Pandawa. A fierce battle ensues and the
Pandawa are defeated. Sakula-Sadewa learn of their brothers' trouble
and rush back home. After exchanging greetings and renewing the
pleasure of one another's company, they set off for the battle field.
The two giants are vanquished and re-transformed in *gandarwa* fairies. They thank Sadewa and make their exit.

The closing scene of the Sudamala *lakon* is a restatement in summary form of all that has gone on before this point. It directs our
attention to the immanent-existential quadrant, or to empirical life
in the real world where the Pandawa defeat signified disequili-
brium. This was quickly rectified by Sakula-Sadewa, ie, the *kawula-
Gusti* relationship, which purged the situation of the evil influence of giants. The *lakon*'s concluding statement was almost
certainly intended to drive home the message that, for the Javanese, the consubstantiation of *kawula* with *Gusti* was the truest,
most powerful and most legitimate relationship.

From the foregoing analysis it can be seen that both knight
(Sadewa) and commoner (Semar) could become one with *Gusti*,

or reach an indeterminable plane 'beyond explanation.' Such a union was highly idealized and became the focus of orientation by virtue of its ability to resolve temporal crises,[16] and deliver humanity from evil forces and from the incubus of divine retribution. In the *wayang* model a *satria* was able to restore a state of cosmological harmony, or peace-prosperity-justice, only if he and the commoners succeeded in consubstantiating with *Gusti*, since it was in this way that the ultimate truth, ie, the fusion of the essential-religious, existential, transcendent and immanent aspects of life would be held in perfect balance.

The *wayang* also posted beacons of how this focus of orientation was to be reached. In meditation scenes (staged after midnight), a young *satria* would be shown receiving instruction in the code of chivalrous behavior towards the common people. This was inevitably given by a sage-priest who would have the knight concentrate on the three S's: *sabar,* unperturbed in the face of provocation; *sarèh,* gallant and alert to danger; and *salèh,* loyal to God in thought and deed. In addition, the *satria* were used to transfer to the authority-figures and statesmen of pre-colonial times, the four tenents of the chivalrous tradition: *sugih tanpa banda,* be wealthy without owning anything: *perang tanpa bala,* wage war without commanding an army; *menang tanpa ngasoraké,* be victorious without inflicting defeat; and *wèwèh tanpa kélangan,* be magnanimous without incurring loss. To abide by this code a leader had to be endowed with: the wisdom and justice of a king; the foresight of a soothsayer (ascetic); and the true simplicity of a peasant (Boediardjo 1978:101).

---

16. Here I differ with de Jong (1976) who apparently sees the symbol of the Javanese attitude towards life: withdrawal from the material world, concentration on the subline essence and representation of man as God's earthly representative, as being only in the person of the 'king', as expressed through the chivalrous tradition of the *satria*. Arjuna or Mintarogo. This difference of opinion may be because de Jong specifically bases his analysis on the mystical sect known as Pangestu.

3. The Ideal King

The concept of the oneness of *kawula* and *Gusti* also appeared in the interpretation and organization of life in real (existential) society. In the state, as in any other social organization, there must always be two human elements: the organizer and the organized, the government and its citizens or, within the time-frame of this discussion, the *penggede* and *wong cilik,* the élite and the masses. With respect to the *kawula-Gusti* relationship, king and commoner represented obverse and reverse sides of the same coin, different in secular function but of equal transcendent-essential value (Moertono 1981: 25). Both could become sacred by entering the 'indeterminable' state of *suwung awang uwung* through consubstantiation with *Gusti;* hence the identification of the *dewa-raja*[17] (divine-king) and his complement, the divine-commoner, which did not exist in canonic Hinduism, was completely acceptable in Javanese logic. This consubstantiation was entirely possible because in Javanese mysticism there were certain attributes common to both God and man located within the inexplicable essence and substance of the *suksma* (Sanskrit: soul) or *nur* (Arabic: light).[18] In the identification of divine-king and divine-commoner one finds a veiled expression of the ideal state of *tatatentrem,* since it was only when *kawula* and *Gusti* consubstantiated that the cosmos approached tri-harmonic order. As a result of associating the *kawula-Gusti* concept with the identification of the ideal king, the king's position was fixed at that point where all parts of the existential microcosmos were in conjunction. This point was the seat of omnipotence and absolute

---

17. In his study of *candi*, W. F. Stutterheim (1931) notes the appearance of the *dewa-raja* in Hindu-Javanese internment statuary as a deviation from prevailing concepts in the canons of Indic Hinduism. In *candi* where dead rulers were portrayed in the guise of gods, the builders were probably Javanese who had studied under an Indian *guru,* because the deification of kings is not characteristic of royal statuary in India.

18. See Moertono (1981 : 5) and Susanto (1977 : 27–37).

legitimacy from which cosmological order was either created or restored to equilibrium if it had been disturbed.[19] Had a king ever succeeded in occupying this position, he would have realized the virtually unattainable Javanese ideal and become the king at one with *Gusti*. However, in the ordinary world of mundane existence this position was but an ideal and, as such, functioned more as a field of orientation than anything else, for to have attained a perfect state of harmony with *Gusti*, the king would have had to possess the 'indeterminable' absolute power and legitimacy found at the O-locus[20]. Moreover, any king aiming for this ideal had to have the backing of both his officials and subjects because it was this dimension of the *kawula-Gusti* bond which legitimated his temporal position. By the same token, officials and subjects had to ally themselves with king in an outward display of unity which would show the absolute legitimacy of their sovereign's rule and thus bring about tri-harmonic order. Both of these concepts can be written as:

$$\text{ideal king} = \text{king} \times Gusti = O$$
$$tatatentrem = \text{subjects} \times \text{king} \times Gusti = O$$

It does not seem unreasonable that the Javanese would have wished for the realization of their ideal in the immanent and existential world, but for this to occur the king would have had to be capable of generating and protecting *tatatentrem* from all disturbances whether of essential (epidemics, natural catastrophes) or existential (crime, murder, war) origin. This was a formidible task, one calling for an individual with sufficient force of charac-

19. The king is said to have *mbaudenda nyakrawati:* presided over the whole world and dispensed justice by virtue of his might (Moertono 1981 : 71). See C.C. Berg (1983a) who regards the king as the centre of the state's magical power.
20. The complete emptiness symbolized by the O-locus (*suwung* or consubstantiation with *Gusti*) is also the major theme of the Borobudur. At the core area of the temple (the topmost stupa), one finds just that — absolutely nothing. From the logical progression of statues depicting the seated Budha on lower levels, there should be eight at the top. Setiadijaya (1983) explains this absence mathematically as : $8 \times 0 = 0$.

ter, physical strength and intelligence to dominate the political arena and quickly dispense with any opposition which arose. Physical power alone was not enough, however, because the king also had to deflect supernaturally-induced disturbances, and for this he needed the extraphysical or magical ability derived from the power of *kasekten*.

That both immanent physical power and transcendent *kasekten* were indispensible to the king can be seen from the following two excerpts from the *Babad Tanah Jawi*. The first deals with that part of the investiture ceremony called the *penantang,* or ritual challenge. On this particular occasion Panembahan Senopati's successor, Prince Seda Krapyak (1601–1613), stood before the large assembly that had come to witness his enthronement and grandly issued the following challenge:

> "All people of Mataram, whoever they may be, witness, that at this very day, the crown-prince assumes the sultanship, succeeding his august fath er. If there is anybody who feels dissatisfied in his heart, show your intention now and I will be your opponent in duel." "At this the people of Mataram *assaur peksi djumurung* (hailed it unanimously)" (Moertono 1981: 59).

The second excerpt explains the workings of extraphysical *kasekten* during a natural catastrophe thought to have been the result of supernatural forces. When Mt. Merapi erupted in 1672:

> "The mountain heaved in an ominous, primordial rumble, spewing fire from its gaping mouth. Boulders collided in mid-air raining showers of sparks onto the countryside below. Volcanic bilge boiled down rivers and up over their banks, entombing whole villages for all eternity. Slag and cinder slushing through the streets of the capital (of Mataram) harrassed the terrified populace. Only when the King had commanded the Learned (*ulama* and *haji)* to pray to Allah did Merapi's anger subside" (Labberton 1921: 200).

These two excerpts provide a zoom-view of the king interacting with his people to achieve a specific aim. In the *penantang* the king's show of potential force was intended to rally the people behind him, to acknowledge the legitimacy of his succession, and thus head off any dissension during the critical period when responsibility for the order of the state was changing hands. The eruption excerpt serves to illustrate how the fusion of royal power and the religious authority of the *ulama* was believed to produce enough *kasekten* to contact and invoke the Almighty Will of Allah to subdue the volcano.

However, the relation between temporal and extraphysical power was, as one might expect, paradoxical. The unrelenting pressure on the king to enlarge his power-base meant that he had to gain control of an ever greater share of material – including human – resources but this could only be effected by 1) exploiting the people and, 2) embarking on military compaigns to expand territory. While such strategums may have enchanced the king's immanent power, they would also have alienated him from his people and thus loosened the *kawula-Gusti* bond. Moreover, the pursuit of materiality had the effect of taking the king further away from the accumulation of extraphysical power because the conditions for acquiring transcendent *kasekten* were such that the king had to reject everything implied by temporality, and instead seek spiritual purity through a regime of ascesis and observance of religious rituals. Thus, the king was neatly caught in a logic trap, and the only means of extracting him from the paradox of having to amass both transcendent and immanent power was to orient these towards the centripetal O-locus, the union of *kawula* and *Gusti*, where even the most inexplicable anomalies could be accomodated[21]. The harmonious co-existence of both seemingly incompatible types of power can be drawn as:

---

21. This process was formulated in one concept known as *eling,* the gist of which is that everyone had to remember where he had come from in order to know what he should be doing next. When people forgot Who had brought them into the world, they planted the seeds of their own anomie (see Koentjaraningrat 1957 : 77). The same proceedure was called *kawi-caksanaan* when it referred to one's official position. In this case it meant the intelligence required to access each situation correctly and deal justly with all concerned (Moertono 1981 : 40–41), and was often mentioned in conjunction with the king's expertise in appointing his ministers.

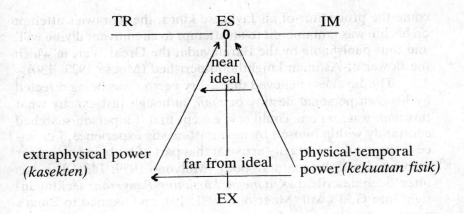

Figure 6. The Javanese Ideal King.

Had this immanent-transcendent reconciliation not been allowed for, the king would have been forced to function at half-strength, since he could not have protected the state from both its natural and supernatural foes at the same time. Even when equiped with physical and extraphysical power, the king still did not have all the prerequisites needed to get him to O, because his position in the microcosmic order was, like everyone else's, subject to essential-immanent factors identified variously as: *titah, takdir,* and *wahyu*[22]. Such factors were held to have been instrumental in the course of human life since man first began to inhabit the natural world. In *wayang* mythology Parikesit, the Pandawa son of Abimanyu who succeeded Suyudana as king of Astina, was said to have been infused with *wahyu*. Since Parikesit was destined to be-

---

22. The Javanese conceived of *wahyu* as an aurora of divine origin irradiating kingship. It was a substance of intense energy attracted to the 'force field' created during meditation and capable of entering the human body. It was believed to move from the body a dead king to that of another chosen by God. The fact that *wahyu* was mobile and divine meant that kingship was extremely vulnerable to the possibility of illegal change (Moertono 1981 : 40–41).

come the progenitor of all Javanese kings, the Korawa's attempt on his life was tantamount to an attempt to circumvent divine will, and thus punishable by the Baratayuda, the Great War, in which the flower of Astinian knighthood perished (Moesa 1923: 130).

The Javanese believed that every person was being directed by his own personal destiny or *titah,* although just exactly what this *titah* was, no one could say, except that if a person searched constantly within himself by means of mystic experience, i.e., ascesis, he would eventually arrive at that part of his being no longer associated with his material body (Mulyono 1979: 143). This has often been described as *maneges karsaning Pangeran:* seeking insight into God's will (Moertono 1981: 19), and likened to Bima's quest in the Dewaruci *lakon*[23].

There was, however, no way that the king could openly point to his destiny as proof of the legitimacy of his position; this could only be done by bringing the country to the threshold of tri-harmonic order where *kawula* and *Gusti* were perfectly united. The *Babat Tanah Jawi* describes Panembahan Seda Krapyak (of the *panantang*) as a devout king whose rule was justice itself (Moertono 1981: 51), but as such virtue was probably very rare or even impossible to emulate under real conditions, the Javanese compensated with a variety of religious ceremonials: ritual commensality, *garebeg*[24], and offertory *labuhan* processions made to Mt.

---

23. The Dewaruci *lakon* describes Bima's struggle to find the essence of this being. In the end he happens upon a miniature replica of himself at the bottom of the sea. Interestingly enough, Dewaruci is now the name of a well-know Indonesian naval vessel.

24. *Garebeg* are offertory ceremonials intended to unify all strata in society, and are still held three times a year : *Garebeg Maulud,* to celebrate the birth of the Prophet Mohammed; *Garebeg Besar,* to honour the legendary Islamic saints, Hasan and Husain; and *Garebeg Puasa,* to express thanks at the close of the fasting month of Ramadan. The core of the *garebeg* is like that of the *selamatan,* ie, a communal meal (*convivium*), but it is held on a much larger scale and attended by huge crowds. On these occasions a huge pyramid of cooked rice is carried in procession from the sultan's palace to the Great Mosque, blessed by Islamic ecclesiastics and then distributed among all those present (see Groneman 1895 : and Soemardjan 1981 : 33).

Merapi and the South Java Sea. These ceremonials were, however, too much of a communal affair to afford the king the opportunity of demonstrating that he, and he alone, was destined to lead his country into the ideal state. The most customary way for the king to legitimate his temporal position was to establish a link between himself and either a ruler from the halcyon days of the glorious past or a supernatural being, such as Nyai Rara Kidul, the goddess of the South Ocean. The principle underlying such a link was a manifestation of continuity between the 'indeterminable subject' and an existential individual. Unlike *wahyu,* this particular testimony of the king's right to rule was overt because whatever had been integrated with 'the indeterminable subject' (O) automatically became 'indeterminable', too. One example of how Javanese kings took maximum advantage of this overtness was the 'state-of-the-art' techniques used in compiling royal genealogies. As mentioned before, the Javanese had a cognatic kinship system and were able to claim both patrilineal and matrilineal descent. The system was unusual in that ancestry could be traced not only through consanguinity, which is objective, but also through mythological lineages, which is cultural. Both techniques were legitimate and acceptable provided that they allowed the people to perceive their king as the one rightfully chosen to fulfil his divine destiny. It is not surprising then that Javanese kings seem to have been able to compile whatever sort of genealogy they wished[25]. The principle of continuity with the 'indeterminable

---

25. Royal genealogies bifurcated into a left *(panengen)* and right *(pangiwa)* branch. The right branch began with Kanjeng Rasul (Mohammed), ran through numerous saints and ended with Amangkurat III; the left began with the Prophets Adam and Sis (Islamic), extended through the major Hindu gods, went on to King Watugunung and the more illustrious of the Pandawa, and ended with Javanese kings from the Majapahid through Mataram eras (Moertono 1981 : 58–59; see also de Graff 1970). Pigeaud (1927 : 346) associates these branches with a classification system in which *panengen* ancestors would belong to the group of olds and *pangiwa* to the youngs. As the ideal king would have been able to use both branches at the same time, this would put him outside the old: young dichotamy, and right at the centre.

subject' may help explain why consanguinity was not strictly adhered to in questions of royal succession, and why the Javanese so readily accepted the claims of successors who were not direct and natural lineal descendents of the previous ruler. It also explaints why leaders of rebellions (Heine-Geldern 1956: 7–11) or of charismatic, ie, *Gusti*-inspired, movements of a revolutionary character would have had such easy access to the kingship (Kartodirjo 1970: 7). The fact that aristocratic titles do not appear to have been granted according to any hard and fast rules may also be due to the same principle. The title *radèn* is an excellent case in point; those related to the royal family through birth or marriage were permitted to bear this title, but since functionaries holding high administrative posts were also called *radèn* a commoner could inherit or marry into the same title as an aristocrat (Koentjaraningrat 1957: 7–8).

A closer look at the custom of legitimating kingship through continuity with a golden era in the past reveals two very interesting facts. The first is the emphasis placed on the revitalizing effect of marriage in the formation of a new dynasty; one recurrent theme in panegyrical chronicles is the legitimation of a new royal house through marriage to a woman having this sort of magical power. For instance, when Ken Arok, the first king of Singosari, was trying to find someone to carry on his line, he was advised to marry Tunggul Ametung's wife, Ken Dedes[26], because the glow emanating from her womb was a sure sign that the child she carried was destined to be a king (Moertono 1981: 54). The second point to note is the tendency for chroniclers to date the fall and rise of dynasties with chronogrammatic phrases ending in the digits '00 – '03 (Ricklefs 1973: 273–346). The disappearance of Brawijaya, the last king of Majapahit, is recounted in the *Babad Keraton* (stanzas 12–14)as follows:

---

26. *C.C. Berg (in Bosch 1956 : 7) draws an analogy between this marriage and that of Batara Guru and Uma (Durga) to show that the Arok-Dedes and Guru-Durga myths are homologous.*

12. All the troops of Bintara
    had reached the Ruler of Majapahit
    As for him, he knew
    the Ruler would be changed
    by the Lord God Most High.
    Mutually looking at one another,
    (Brawidjaja) and Adipati Bintara,

13. Brawidjaja disappeared and was gone,
    with his wives and the *patih* Gadjah Mada,
    the sound thundering,
    disappearing from the kraton.
    Adipati Bintara spoke softly,
    'My Father was the Buddhist Ruler,
    his death true gnosis'.

14. 'Disappeared, gone, the feeling of the world,'
    in the chronogram for the fall of Madjapahit.
    All the Royal possessions
    were laid out there,
    those that were *pusakas,* all,
    and the treasures
    were laid out in the Presence.

    (Ricklefs 1972: 301–302)

In the fourteenth stanza the disappearance of Brawijaya is dated with the chronogram: *sirna ilang rasa duniawinya,* ie, 1600 *Saka,* but the real meaning of this particular phrase is still not clear. It is generally held that Majapahit fell in 1400 *Saka* (1475 A.D.), not 1600, and in fact another chronogram: *sirna ilang rasaning ingkang bumi,* which also means 1600 *Saka,* has been used to date the fall of Plered (Ricklefs 1972: 314).

Ricklefs argues that the last two digits in the chronogram, i.e., '00, were related to the notion that a change of century also represented a change of dynasty (1973: 314). Another interpretation[27] is that these digits stood for an age, and not for a year, in which case dynastic change may have been connected with the Hindu cosmological view of the universe as being in a constant state of cyclical change involving four different *yuga* (ages): *Kertayuga-Tretayuga-Dwaparayuga-Kaliyuga*. In classical Javanese thought, the end for a dynasty was associated with the ominous *Kalabendu* or *Kaliyuga*,[28] the fourth and most terrible age in the cycle, after which the universe entered the halcyonic prosperity of *sirna* (0), or heaven (Drewes 1925: 164–168). The words *sirna ilang* ('00) may possibly have been intended to mark the end of the *Kalabendu* Age, or they may have meant that Majapahit fell after this age[29]. Research into whether the other two digits often found in chronogrammatic phrases, ie, '03, can be interpreted as an early sign of the rise of a new dynasty is still inconclusive. This is pure speculation, but the words for '03 may have been used to

---

27. These digits are open to a number of different interpretations, especially in view of the fact that the description of the past found in chonicles could very well have been mythological (see Drewes 1939 : 247 and 249; see also Djajadiningrat 1913).

28. The *Kaliyuga* or *Kali* Age takes its name from the cannibal-king, Batara Kala, who was reincarnated in the form of Kaliyuga: *Narendra naramangsa pawak i titah nikang Kaliyuga* (Zoetmulder 1982 : 778). In the Sutasoma myth the malevolent Batara Kala vows to devour 100 kings. Sutasoma offers to sacrifece himself that the other kings, the realm and religon might be saved. Kala agrees but later has a change of heart, repents his evil ways and, instead of eating Sutasoma, decides to study under him. At the end, Sutasoma and his wife depart from the world and ascend into Jina heaven leaving their son, Andhana, to rule the kingdom of Astina (Zoetmulder 1974 : 341).

29. Note the homology between Sutasoma's ascension into Jina and Brawijaya's disappearnce in stanza 12 of the *Babad Keraton*.

date the emergence of a new dynasty in the *Dwaparayuga*,[30] the third age. If this could be proved, then the *Dwapara* Age could be written into the Javanese kingship model[31] in the third or immanent-existential quadrant, since this is where life was seen as entering the concrete, material world or where, by homology, a new dynasty would make an appearance.

To conclude this section it only remains to mention a few other methods of legitimating kingship. The first involved the collection of *pusaka*[32], dwarfs and albinos about the person of the king, as these were believed to be intrinsically powerful and would, therefore, have enchanced his transcendent *kasekten*. The king also sought to overtly legitimate his rule by other material means: accumulating personal wealth, amassing large numbers of kin, and commanding great civilian and military populations. However, the Javanese would never have considered this method of legitimation an end in itself because the majesty (*keluhuran*) of the king was always associated with his inner greatness (*keagungan*). It was said that lesser men paid homage to a truly great king, not because military defeat or fear had forced them to do so, but rather because they could not hold out in the face of such benevolent justice and wisdom. In fact, the misuse or royal prerogative for purely material gain was taken as a sign that the king's *wahyu* was about to depart and the end of his reign would swiftly follow (Moertono 1981: 73).

---

30. *Dwapara:* the third age. H.W.52.8: *dwapara tan pangangasan hana sang narendra,* which means that *dwapara* does not deny the exissence of the king (Zoetmulder 1982 : 447). The *Hariwangsa* recounts that in the Dwapara Age, Vishnu or Hari (the savior-god) appeared in the avatar Kresna (the Pandawa king, Dwarawati) to tree the world from satonic influences (Zoetmulder 1974 : 225).
31. Transformed model from the model of Javanese logic to kingship. Compare Figure 3. (page) with Figure 5 (page).
32. *Pusaka:* generic name for all manner of palladia comprising mainly fetishtic weaponry (*keris*, lances) and state regalia (thrones, royal coaches).

4. Kingship in Practice.

No attempt has been made to turn this examination of the practical aspects of kingship into a detailed account of historical events. Instead, I have tried to demonstrate the coherence of concepts of ideal kingship by throwing these ideas into relief against a background of historial phenomena relating to political processes and movements aimed at achieving certain ideals, and best exemplified by throne disputes and messianic, or *Ratu Adil,* movements. These were certainly no stranger to the Javanese historical scene, especially in view of the openness characterizing kingship.

A brief look through Javanese history from the fall of Majapahit in the fifteenth century will attest to the tenacity of the traditional ideal of peace-prosperity–justice under a rightful and righteous king. War became the single most constant feature throughout the period of search for the ideal king, the one who would administer Java as one nation and one people. It was perhaps only during the reign of Sultan Agung (1613–1645) that most of Java, excluding Banten and Batavia, came under the sway of one supreme ruler. This brief respite ended with Sultan Agung's death in 1645, after which the kingdom plunged back into the usual round of insurrection and war lasting well into the eighteenth century. To mention only a few better known examples, there was: Trunojoyo's takeover of Mataram's court-city in Plered (1674–77); the first War of Succession between Sunan Mas (Amangkurat III) and his uncle Prince Puger who had VOC (Dutch East Indies Company) backing; the second War of Succession (1719–1723) featuring Amangkurat IV against his relatives; the Chinese Rebellion (1740); the war between the VOC-backed Pakubuwono II and Sunan Kuning; and the third War of Succession with Pakubuwono II and III on one side, and Prince Mangkubumi and Mas Said on the other.

The upshot of the third War of Succession was the Treaty of Gianti and subsequent partitionment of Mataram into the sunanate of Surakarta and sultanate of Yogyakarta. In a second settlement the principality of Mangkunegaran was carved out of Surakartan territory and given to Mas Said. After this contenders for the title, Supreme Ruler of Java, went into limbo and the country drifted into a fitful peace lasting until the close of the nineteenth century. The fact that settling throne disputes through open warfare fell out of fashion may have been partially due to the presence of the VOC as a military force and self-declared mediator in inter-kingdom altercations.

Although the brakes had been applied to open confrontation, king and courtier alike never abandoned the cherished ambition of uniting all of Java under one rule. There were less overt attempts made at reunifying Surakarta and Yogyakarta through diplomatic marriages but these were stillborn. The failure of Prime Minister Danurejo to arrange a marriage between the children of Hamengkubuwono I and Pakubuwono III has been interpreted as a sign of the irrevocable division of Mataram (Ricklefs 1973), Both courts went to considerable effort to give the impression that their separate existences were sanctioned by tradition, but this was no more than an artful bit of blarney concocted mainly to disorient the true undercurrent of traditional belief that Java had to be ruled by a cosmologically legitimate king, at one with *Gusti*. The reality of this sentiment finally gathered enough momentum to express itself in the outbreak of the Diponegoro War, the background of which has been dealt with by a number of historians (Louw and de Klerk 1904; Soekanto 1952; Sagimun 1960 and 1976; Yamin 1950; Carey, 1974, 1976, 1979 and 1981; and Ricklefs 1974). Each analysis of the war has different shades of meaning but these will not be discussed here, except in so far as they have a bearing on a) the situation in the courts of Surakarta-Yogyakarta and role of the Dutch just prior to the war, or b) the character of Prince Diponegoro himself.

Conditions at court in the period leading up to the war were characterized by intrigue and friction between the nobles which set brother against brother and father against son. Much of the disorder can be traced back to the weakness or lack of acumen of incumbent kings. A good example is Sultan Sepuh, who lacked the strength of character required to call a halt to the conflict between his own sons and Prince Natakusuma. He also completely ignored the political advances instituted by Hamengkubuwono I and, in a move of pure retrogression, dismissed most of his older, more experienced advisory staff and replaced them with younger, untried men. Further unrest originated from the women's quarters where competition among each of Sepuh's wives to have her son named crown prince significantly increased the level of tension within the palace. Moreover, there was insufficient land available to outfit the rapidly expanding class of princes and noblemen with appanages large enough to support their extravagant life style. Being reduced to pawning one's land and tenents or leasing them out to the Chinese or to Dutch planters contributed little towards improving the foul mood of the aristocracy.

In a rash move to put the state on a firmer financial footing tax inputs to palace coffers were quadrupled (Carey 1974: 54) between 1792 and 1802, mainly by reducing the size of *cacah* units while holding the amount of tax payable constant[33]. Collection rates were stepped up at tolls and other points of levy to such an extent that a portage duty was imposed on every woman using main roads, regardless of whether her load contained market produce borne in a basket or simply a child slung over the back (Sagimun 1960: 45). In addition to greater tax revenues, Sultan Sepuh claimed an increased share of corvée from peasants in outlying districts for large-scale construction projects, such as palatial hunting lodges. It was in this way that the Sultan disregarded the welfare of his subjects to the point of adding to the wretched misery of their poverty. In terms of the ideal king model, there was a wide

---

33. This system, known as *pancasan* (see Rouffaer 1931 : 14, 75, 85; and Onghokham 1979 : 623), involved using a shorter unit of measurement, ie, the *cengkal* from Majapahit times so that while real hectareage per *cacah* declined, the number of households taxed remained constant or even increased.

gulf between ruler and ruled, because the people, who were without access to material benefits, were in the transendent-existential quadrant, while the king, who controlled all sources of this benefit, was in the immanent – existential quadrant.

Unlike Hamengkubuwono I, Sultan Sepuh had no sense of diplomacy in his dealings with the Dutch. The Dutch may have been prepared to accept arrogance and inflexibility in a ruler when their position was still extremely weak, as was the case during the reign of Hamengkubuwono I, but by the time of Daendels and Raffles this sort of attitude was no longer tolerable (Carey 1974). In fact it was Sepuh's refusal to comply with the decree on 'Ceremony and Etiquette', designed to put Dutch emissaries on a par with the king, which provoked Daendels into attacking Yogyakarta in 1810. Sepuh was deposed and Diponegoro's father, Hamengkubuwono III, came to power. Daendels' reaction further polarized palace factions and served to expose another piece of 'court-politik' to the effect that the Dutch were the legal heirs to the kingdom of Pajajaran with no authority to interfer in matters relating to Javanese succession. Their presence had hitherto been acknowledged as only that of a counterpart government with powers not to exceed beyond the north coast of Java[34].

Sultan Sepuh was not, however, to be so easily dismissed, and in 1811 when the five-year British inter-regnum began, he ousted his son and reinstated himself. Raffles initially sanctioned this move, perhaps out of a sense of gratitude for the part Sepuh had played in helping the British turn the tables on the Dutch, but it was not long before he, too, tired of the Sultan's insolence and

---

34. The *Baron Sakendher* myth was an attempt to rationalize the presence of the Dutch in Java. The general story-line is that the Dutch were really descended from Sukmul, who had come to Jakarta from Spain in search of his twin-brother, Sakendher. This Sukmul married Tanuraga, the magically-born daughter of King Sekar Mandapa of Pajajaran, after learning of this brother's defeat at Senopati's hands. Senopati was the ancestral king of Mataram, and this accounted for the fact that Mataram was more powerful than the Dutch (Pigeaud 1927).

insubordination, and packed him off to exile in Penang. Hameng-kubuwono III then re-ascended the throne, but the area under his command was now considerably smaller because the British had annexed Kedu, and Yogyakarta had been truncated by the formation of the principality of Pakualaman in a repeat performance of what had happened in 1757 when Mangkunegaran was cut away from Surakarta. Raffles' policies, like Daendels' before him, could not but be interpreted as further proof that the government of Yogyakarta was now under the control of a foreign 'king' who had small regard for the people, in terms of either their welfare or their religion.

Hamengkubuwono III's fate was sealed the day Pakualaman was set up as a department in the Raffles' administration, for perhaps the people could have borne anything save for the final ignominy of watching their shining ideal debase himself in the service of the British Crown for 100,000 Spanish dollars a year (Soe-kanto 1952: 96). The following verses from the *Babad Surakarta* capture some of the anomie filling the vacuum at the centre of Yo-gyanese society after the loss of its single focus of spiritual and political power.

> 7. All the *nayakas* (chief advisers) in Yogya
> together without scruple followed their own wishes
> just as they pleased.
> Many of their orders were not authorized,
> numerous old customs were abrogated
> (and) the common people were bewildered.
> There were changes in the direction of the state
> (and) there was much calumny. Bandits, highwaymen,
> robbers and thieves
> could move about in the kingdom.

> 8. The law of the *surambi* was not enforced
> and the administration by the *pradata* (civil court) was fitful.
> All the essential elements of the law were disregarded.
> Arbitrariness prevailed
> and those in authority acted strongly

and in an unsuitable (and) unmannerly fashion.
Many people were dismissed by ruses
(and) in the councils other men took their places,
descendants of common people.

9. Often foodstuffs were scarce and unwholesome.
Many common people fled to other villages
and towns as they wished.
Much of their attachment
for the state and their king disappeared.
The *ricinus* (castor-oil) plant sprang up
(but) the teak tree died
so to speak,
for staid people and gentry
were ousted by intruding upstarts.

(in Carey 1976:71, translated from Lor 2114, I
(Dhandhanggula, p.2)).

When lawlessness and social deterioration continued unabated,
conditions became ripe for the appearance of millenarianism and
the Javanese messianic tradition of the *Ratu Adil* (Righteous
King). Prince Diponegoro would undoubtably have been aware of
the mood of the times, and may even have exploited it to gain
popular support for his own cause. And, while Diponegoro's
insurrection assumed different proportions as it developed into
the Java War (1825–1830), this does not detract from the fact that
his original decision to rebel stemmed from a personal vandetta
with the Dutch.

Diponegoro was Hamengkubuwono III's eldest son, but
because his mother was a concubine, the British would not recog-
nise him as heir apparent. When the old sultan died, the British
overrode his claim and had Jarot, the son of an official wife and
Diponegoro's junior by eighteen years, named Sultan
Hamengkubuwono IV. While this is thought to have deeply
offended Diponegoro (Soekanto 1952: 100), the extent to which it
influenced his plans for rebellion is really beside the point. As far

as my analysis is concerned, it sufficient to note that he was a high-ranking noble capable of quickly raising a good deal of support among the various factions at court.

It is somewhat unusual for the cloying atmosphere of the court to have produced an individual of Diponegoro's calibre. However, it should be remembered that he spent his formative years away from palace and, apart from putting in perfunctory appearances at *garebeg* festivals, generally eschewed court life[35]. From the time he was six years old he had lived with Ratu Ageng, his great-grandmother and wife of Hamengkubuwono I (Sagimun 1976: 62). Here he received a broad-based Islamic education, becoming well-versed in Islam law and Koranic exegis, and making contacts among the Islamic teachers, theologians and orthodox Muslims in Yogyakarta (Carey 1979: 64). He had a deep affinity for Javanese mysticism and immersed himself in esoteric writings, classical literature and historiographies of the old Mataram kingdom. It is quite likely that he tried to model himself after the legendary Arjuna[36] because his ascetic pursuits followed a pattern similar to those of the Pandawa knight before embarking on the Baratayuda War (Ricklefs 1974: 230).

Judging from Diponegoro's upbringing, he would probably have been equally at ease in both the Islamic and Javanese world, and have had little difficulty in synthesizing the two. His own autobiography, the *Serat Babad Diponegoro,* written after his exile to Menado in 1830, attests to the syncretic philosophical basis of experiences inspiring his revolt against the Dutch. My analysis of these experiences is taken from Ricklefs' work (1974) on the first 27 stanzas of this autobiography.

---

35. In court tradition any prince choosing to live away from court could be accused of refusing to acknowledge the authority of the reigning king and labeled a *kraman,* ie, a dissident and rebel.
36. Both the *Serat Babad Diponegoro* and *Kedhung Kebo* mention the *Arjuna Wijaya.* In Rifklefs' opinion (1974), Diponegoro's character was closer to Arjuna in the classic *Arjuna Wiwaha* (Arjuna's Wedding) and thus differed considerably from the one portrayed in the *Arjuna Wijaya.*

Diponegoro's spiritual awakening began under the influence of his great-grandmother who introduced him to a religious ethic pledged to protect the faithful. By the age of twenty he had become so deeply involved with Islam that he could no longer reconcile religious committment with secular loyalty to Sultan Sepuh (stanza 3), and consequently only came to court for the *garebeg*. Occasional as these contacts were, they made him feel sinful (stanza 4)[37], but he was still too afraid of the Sultan and his father to completely dispense with them. Diponegoro's reluctance to sever all ties with the palace indicates that he was as yet unprepared to force a situation of open conflict with the Sultan. This indecision is also reflected in the fact that he used his Javanese name, Pangeran Diponegoro, at court and his Islamic name, Seh Ngabdurahkim, outside the capital (stanza 5). His use of two names may have been part of a tactical manoeuver to satisfy palace etiquette without compromising his religious principles[38]. Above all he longed for spiritual purity and although often tempted to break his vow of chastity (stanza 6), struggled to remain true to his ideals. Reflecting on the higher truth of his existence (*wekasan dumadi*), he travelled incognito from mosque to mosque where he aligned himself with orthodox *santri* who were generally more ascetically-inclined (stanza 7). He found himself drawn especially to the suffering commoners who moved about among Islamic minor seminaries (*pesantren*).When he grew weary of this itinerant way of life he retreated into the cool of the forests and mists of high places, staying in caves or wandering along deserted beaches (stanzas 8–9).

---

37. Palmer van den Broek's interpretation (in Ricklefs 1974 : 231) is probably more accurate.

38. From this desire to synthesize secular authority with a religious life style it will become clear that Diponegoro was attempting to recreate the *Arjuna Wiwaha* written in the eleventh century as an analogical biography of Erlangga. Mpu Kanwa's classic portrays Arjuna or Erlangga as a new king who restores peace and prosperity after managing to combine the virtue of a pious sage with the valour of a military commander (C.C. Berg 1938 : 26–46).

Diponegoro's first encounter with the supernatural occurred in Sor Kamal cave during the sacred month of Ramadan. In the middle of the night God sent many visions to test him, but when his concentration did not waver, the temptations finally ceased to disturb him. Then the Islamic saint, Sunan Kalijaga, appeared to him saying: "God (Hyang Suksma) has willed that you, Ngabdul-rahkim, are to be King (Ratu Ngerang-erang)" (stanza 11). Before the starled Prince had time to kneel before him, the saint had vanished. Following this, Diponegoro's spiritual quest led him to the royal cemetary at Imogiri where he spent a week in prayer and contemplation at the grave of Sultan Agung, from whom all Javanese kings, including himself, were descended (stanzas 13–15). A visit to the ancestral graves can be construed as an attempt to discover the clarity of mind needed to provide physical and mental powers. This has been compared to following a river back to its source: the closer one gets to the source, the clearer the water [39]. By the same token, a person tracing his lineage will find that the further back he goes, the greater the clarity, ie, purity, of his ancestors' blood-lines. It is quite conceivable that Diponegoro would have turned to his ancestors for clarity of inspiration when conditions in the kingdom became so unsettled as to have clouded the vision of his purpose. However, as Diponegoro's autobiography holds no clue of why he actually went to Imogiri, this is all purely conjecture on my part.

From Imogiri Diponegoro headed south and spent two nights in the caves at Sagala-gala before going on to the Langse grotto overlooking the South Java Sea.[40] Here he passed a half-month in prayer and fasting (stanza 17), trying to clear his mind, to peel back successive layers of consciousness, before emerging into the 'indeterminable' emptiness of *suwung* (stanza 18). When Nyai Rara Kidul came, he was too far into his being to see the goddess of the South Ocean, although he did hear her promise to

---

39. Oral information provided by Fr. Kuntara Wiryamartana S.J.
40 Even today Langse is still a favoured Yogyanese meditation spot.

return when his time was at hand (stanzas 19–20). At daybreak he was again aware of his natural surroundings; he walked to Parang Tritis and then over to Parang Kusuma where he bathed.

He was meditating next to a rock when he heard a far-off voice say that he was to became the guardian of Java and, to help him carry out this mission, he would be given Arjuna's magical arrow, Sarotama (stanza 22). The voice also instructed him to return home and to reject any Dutch proposals to name him Prince Dipati [41]. Upon opening his eyes he found himself alone. As he looked up he saw something streak through the sky and land in front of him. It was the sacred Sarotama shaft; he picked it up and started for home (stanza 25).

The voices Diponegoro heard on the south coast leave little doubt that the purpose of his impending struggle with the Dutch was to reunify Java and purge it of all colonial influences since, according to Javanese kingship theory, it was only in this way that the ideal of *tatatentrem* would be attained (see page on the appearance of a new dynasty after the *Kalabendu* Age). To this end he was forbidden to acknowledge Dutch authority, and instructed to resist any overtures to make him their vassal. Ricklefs (1974: 246) takes this to mean that Diponegoro was to avoid having his name associated with any other Dutch moves to partition Java.

In general, Diponegoro's ascesis represents a consistent working out of the kingship tradition model: he struggled to separate himself from material existence and move towards the 'indeterminable' O-locus, ie, the consubstantiation of *kawula* and *Gusti,* as part of his quest for the kingship [43]. He also succeeded in *neges karsaning Pangeran:* responding to his call or destiny as handed down through the traditional supernatural figures of Sunan Kalijaga, Nyai Rara Kidul and the mysterious voices. As proof

---

41. This title may have meant that the Dutch wanted to make him an independent prince, as had been done in the case of Pakualam and Mangkunegara (Ricklefs 1974 : 246).
43. I concur with Ricklefs (1974 : 248) on this point.

that he had found a way into the essential-immanent quadrant, and was following his cosmologically legitimate destiny he inherited Sarotama, a palladium from Arjuna, the cerebral and valiant Pandawa knight. Diponegoro's endeavour to consistently apply the principle of *manunggaling kawula-Gusti* is also seen from his actions at the beginning of his campaign against the Dutch (1825) when he had his wife divide all their gold, diamonds and precious stones among his followers (Sagimun 1960: 73). In this way he voided himself of materiality and, in empathizing with the common people who also had no control over material resources, exhibited the attributes of piety and nobility embodied in the Javanese idealization of the *Ratu Adil*. As a result, he soon attracted a mass following from many walks of life: peasants, noblemen, devout Muslims and even the *jago,* the champions, or culture heroes, of the little people. It was, however, due to the paradox of Diponegoro's pursuit of power and materiality, i.e., war, that he returned to the immanent-existential aspects of life. He did in fact become commander-in-chief of the army, but he lost the laurel of *Ratu Adil* and in the end was banished to Menado.

The course of the war from 1925 to 1830 and reasons for Diponegoro's defeat need not be discussed here; suffice it to say that after this point the colonial goverment had complete access to Java. A number of sunanates and sultanates were annexed by the Dutch and one of these was Bagelen, whose traditions I propose to discuss next.

III. THE VILLAGE

1. Bagelen's Position in the Layout of Mataram.

In 1830 Bagelen was a newly-established Dutch residency. It had originally been administered by Surakarta and Yogyakarta but was signed over to the Dutch on 22 June 1830 several months after the Java War ended (TNI 1858: 65). By 1 August Bagelen had ceased to exist: it was struck from official registers and incorporated into the residency of Kedu (ENI). However, in the eyes of its people Bagelen was still a separate entity. When Bagelen's official status was still that of a residency, it comprised the *afdeeling* (sub-residency) of Purworejo, Kebumen and Wonosobo, all of which later became regencies. During the Materam era, only the *afdeeling* of Purworejo and Kebumen had been part of Bagelen; Wonosobo was a separate unit encompassing Ledok and Gowong (Doorn 1926: 3).

Bagelen 'used to be' located in the centre of southern Java, just a few degrees off the equator: 109° 21′ – 1°11′ east latitude by 7° – 7°57′ south latitude (Veth 1809: 44). It was bounded by Pekalongan to the north, Yogyakara and Kedu to the east, the South Java Sea, Banyumas to the southwest, and Tegal to the west. In 1830 Bagelan comprised an area of 2,544 *palen*[2], or approximately 3,831 km², with a total population of 238,764 or 39,794 *cacah*[1].

Bagelen was flanked on three sides by mountain ranges. The Kendeng Mountains extending from east to west along the northern border had two branches: the Kelirs running south along the eastern border at Yogyakarta and the Karang Bolongs, again running south but along the western border at Banyumas. Lowland Bagelen was largely swamp plain lying between the Kelir and

---

1. One paal (palen) = 1,506,000 m (ENI Paal : 226). One *cacah* = 6 persons (TNI 1858).

Karang Bolong ranges. The large eastern Wawar swamp plain, often called *Groote Rawa,* was approximately 11 *palen* long and 2-4 *palen* wide; the western Tambak Baya swamp plain with an area of only 4 by 5 *palen* was considerable smaller. Both plains were flecked with small villages supporting themselves by swampland agriculture during the dry season. Villages along the south coastal swamp plain formed one long, unbroken line (4x40 palen^2) beginning in the east at the village of Kadilangu on the Bagawanta river and ending in the west at the Cincing Guling river in the Karang Bolong foothills. Due to its length, this linear progression of villages came to be known as *Urut Sewu* (lit: one thousand in a row), and is said to have acted as a natural embankment between swamp and sea (TNI 1958: 68).

Very little reliable toponymic information is available for Bagelen. I have chosen A. van Poel's version (1846: 175–176) of the etimology of the name Bagelen not because I intend to analyse it at any great length, but simply because it provides a more detailed description than most. Poel's etimology was compiled from information supplied by several *kentol,* as Bagelen's local gentry were called.

According to these *kentol,* a king's son named Awu-Awu Langit had once farmed a tract of land up in the Kelir Mountains. He was married to Nyai Roro Rengganis [2], a weaver of cloth, and had three children. One day when Awu-Awu was busy filling the family granary, his wife noticed that two of the children were missing. She asked her husband whether he had seen them, to which he replied: "Women, if you paid as much attention to our children as to your precious weaving, you wouldn't be asking me such a question." They bickered a while and then set off to look for the children. After a long and fruitless search the weary couple returned home. They rested and then set off again, but this time

---

2. Another version has it that Nyai Roro Rengganis, who later became Nyai Bagelen, was the granddaughter of Kandihawan, king of all Java and an avatar of Vishnu (TNI 1860 : 207).

their steps took them to the granary. They dumped out some of the rice and there lay the children, quite dead, smothered under the rice. They had been sleeping in the granary unbeknownst to their father when he filled it earlier that day. The couple quarrelled constantly after the death of the children until, unable to stand it any longer, Roro Rengganis asked that Awu-Awu divorce her. This done, Awu-Awu left the farm taking his only surviving child while his wife stayed on, grief-stricken and full of remorse. This feeling is expressed in Javanese with the word *kepegelen,* which also means pains and aches in the limbs. After a period of mourning Roro Rengganis walked off into the west and was never seen again[3]; legend states that she went to heaven. The village she left behind together with area through which she passed was given the name Kepegelen, and eventually came to be called Bagelen.

In order to get a conceptual fix on Bagelen in 1830 when the colonial goverment decided to 'take up residence', it would be best if I explained something of its position within the overall design of the Mataram kingdom. From earlier descriptions of the basic structure of Javanese society as reflected in the kingship tradition, we can assume that pre-colonial society was oriented towards a paradoxical centre symbolized by Semar, the *kawula-Gusti* relationship, and 'indeterminable' emptiness of *suwung awang-uwung.* The concept of the ideal king was based on the same sort of orientation, and consequently the king was located at the intersection of all relations aspiring towards both essential macrocosmic harmonic order (*tatatentrem*) and existential micro-

---

3. It is interesting that Roro Rengganis disappeared in the west, as opposed to some other direction. This may have been connected with the people's desire to show that the Bagelen region began at the village by the same name and extended far to the west. Moreover, and this will be discussed later, the whole sentence may have been a concrete representation of the structure of pre–colonial logic. The west was regarded as a transition point in the journey of life, which began in the east and moved toward a northern point where death occurred.

cosmic order (see page 37-38). It was hoped that as a result of this position the king would have a central role in all activities intended to bring about temporal, i.e., social order. It is not suprising then that the king should, at least conceptually, have occupied so central a position in the spacial organization of the state as the territorial division of Mataram would seem to indicate. In terms of the concept of state administration, Mataram displayed a classic pattern of concentricity [4]:

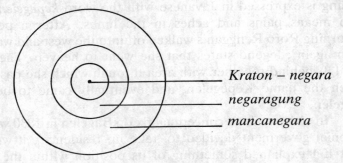

Figure 7. Conceptual Territorial Division of Mataram.

The king, as the nucleus, was surrounded by three ever-widening shells: the *keraton-negara, negara* and *negaragung,* whose attraction to the centre was directly proportional to their distance from it. The *keraton,* or palace, and *negara* functioned as both the lodestone and capital of the kingdom. The *negara* was a vast, walled complex of buildings and squares housing such high-ranking officials as the *patih* (prime minister), *wedana* (head-regent) and *nayaka* (chief administrator). The *negaragung,* or core area of the kingdom, was actually little more than an extension of the *negara* and parcelled into: 1) *mahosan dalem,* ie, crownlands paying taxes directly to the palace, and 2) *lungguh* or

---

4. Selo Soemardjan (1981 : 27); see also Rouffaer (1931) and Burger (1939).

appanages from which officials living within the *negara* drew their income. The *mancanegara,* the third and the largest part of the kingdom, comprised outlying districts intended as an additional source of palace revenue, and was therefore not parcelled into appanages for the benefit of the *priyayi.*

While it is quite correct to say that Mataram was conceptually divided into concentric spheres, especially in so far as administration was concerned [5], a brief objective examination of its spacial organization will reveal an east-west progression of geopolitical units extending in either direction from the *negara* at the centre. Working from information found in the *Serat Raja Puwara,* F.A. Sutjipto has established a clear east-west classification of territory within Mataram's jurisdiction (1980: 30). Since the reign of Sultan Agung the *negaragung* had been divided into eight districts; Bumi (Kedu, west of the Praga river); Bumija (Kedu, east of the Praga); Siti-Ageng Kiwa (on the right or western side of the Pajang-Demak road); Siti-Ageng Tengen (on the left or eastern side of the Pajang-Demak road); Sewu (Bagelen, in the western section of the Bagawanta-Donan Cilacap watershed); Numbak-Anyar (in the eastern section of the Bagawanta-Praga watershed); Panumping (Sukowati); and Panekar (Pajang). When these eight regions are lined up in pairs along the east-west axis of the *negara,* four will be found to lie to the east: Siti-Ageng Kiwa, Siti Ageng Tengen, Panumping, Paneker and four to the west: Bumi, Bumija, Sewu, Numbak-Anyar.

. Land within the *mancanegara* also showed a general east-west pattern of division. The eastern *mancanegara* comprised: Panaraga, Kadiri, Madiun, Pacitan, Kaduwang, Magetan, Caruban, Pace, Kersana, Sarengat, Blitar, Jipang, Garobogan,

---

5. Mataram's concentric system of administration can be seen from the fact that there were four *njero*-regents directly under the prime miniter (Rouffaer 1931 : 55–56). This system paralleled the one operating in Majapahit and Malacca (Kartodirdjo 1964 : 28–29).

64

Warung, Sela, Blora, Rawu (Tulungagung), Barebeg, Jagaraga, Kalangbret, Japan (Majakerta), and Wirasaba (Majaagung). Included in the western *mancanegara* were: Banyumas, Banjar Pasir (Purwakarta), Ngayah, Roma (Karanganyar), Karangbolong, Merden, Warah, Tersana, Karencang, Bobotsari, Kartanegara, Lebak-Siyu, Balapulang, Bentar and Dayaluhur.

In addition to the *negaragung* and *mancanegara*, Mataram's jurisdiction extended to the *pesisir,* the territory running along the north coast of Java. The *pesisir* also appears to have been divided into an eastern section (Pasisiran Wetan) and a western section (Pasisiran Kulon), both of which went in opposite directions starting at Demak [6]. With this last piece of territory accounted for it is now possible to represent the layout of Mataram as a linear progression extending from east to west:

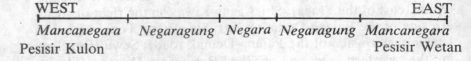

Figure 8. Objective Territorial Division of Mataram.

This horizontal structure is still not completely representative of Javanese spacial concepts as it shows only those pairs of co-ordinates lying along the east-west axis of the kingdom. I have not ventured a description of co-ordinates along a vertical axis because Mataram was an interior kingdom in southern Java and, as such, had no northern or southern tracts of land with a length comparable to that of its territories in the east and west. Since it would have been impossible to apply the same objective principle of geo-polar opposition to delineate north-south territories as in

6. The north coast was not well-integrated with the interior *(negaragung – mancanegara)* and thus not regarded as a central part of the kingdom (Rouffaer 1931 : 48).

the case of east-west territories[7], the Javanese were forced to create illusionary (cultural) northern and southern domains, ie, Mt. Merapi in the north and the South Java Sea. Both of these were perceived as magical kingdoms ruled by supernatural beings, i.e., Kyai Sapujagad and Nyai Rara Kidul, which were united with Mataram's objective east-west territories by Javanese kings[8].

This unification of the kingdom's objective east-west structure with its cultural and mythological north-south structure produced a spacial configuration conforming with the idea of symmetrical wholeness in Javanese cosmology. Pigeaud (1977) points out that Javanese thought has been continuously supported by the perception of cosmic oneness and marked by an aptitude for classification. The universe represented a community where human beings and material existence were locked into intimate contact with all animate and inanimate objects surrounding them. The idea of cosmic co-ordination–interrelation brings to mind a conversation I once had with another Javanese. He remarked that we always identify something by saying what it is not, rather than what it is. He used the days of the week as an analogy: "Isn't today different from yesterday, and won't it be different from to-

---

7. With the exception of the names given to the large palace squares, i.e., Alun-Alun Lor and Alun-Alun Kidul, the north:south category was virtually unexpressed at the concrete, structural level of the kingdom. Since the more common spacial dychotomies were *njaba:njero* (outer:inner); *kiwo:tengen* (left:right); and *wetan:kulon* (east:west), this would indicate that north:south was a latent categorization appearing mostly on a mythological plane.

8. In Javanese logic there was nothing at all unreasonable about the idea that the king should act as a relay between the goddess of the South Ocean and Kyai Supujagad on Mt. Merapi. Even today an annual *Saparan* (propitiatory ceremony in Sapar, the second month in the Islamic calendar) is held in the village of Wonokromo near Plered, 10 km south of Yogyakarta. The *Saparan* always takes place at the confluence of the Opak and Gadjahwong rivers, the exact point of mythological rendezvous between Rara Kidul and Sultan Agung. Incidently, the source of both rivers is on Mt. Merapi.

morrow. All Javanese know this, for why else have they decided that one day should be called *Legi* and another *Paing* and so on?" He continued with another piece of home-spun theorizing: "Is it so unlikely that the difference in our days (read: temporal concepts) fits in with, or has even become the reason for, other differences, such as the fact that everyone is born with their own special character?"

These questions were undoubtably conditioned by the conviction that all elements in the microcosmos relate to one another in harmonic unity. It is possible to give concrete expression to this idea by means of mutually corresponding, congruent classification sets. Correspondences will occur at each point where a fixed relation can be established between one component in one classification set and another component in a different set. Examples of a number of these correspondences are provided in Table1 1[9]. From this table it will be seen that there is a correspondence between the way space was divided according to the cardinal points and the way in which the five-day Javanese week was broken up. The classification: east ≠ south ≠ west ≠ north ≠ centre, parallels that of: *Legi* ≠ *Paing* ≠ *Pon* ≠ *Wage* ≠ *Kliwon* [10]. The homology between the differences in these two classification sets can then be shown as:

east ≠ south ≠ west ≠ north ≠ centre

I   I   I   I

Legi ≠ *Paing* ≠ *Pon* ≠ *Wage* ≠ *Kliwon*

**Figure 9. Homology Between Spacial and Temporal
Classification Sets.**

Given the fact that the Javanese consistently used the principle of congruent correspondence in fashioning other classifacation sets (Pigeaud 1977), it would not be unreasonable to suppose that the

---

9. Similar correspondences are found in narrative form in the Manik Maya story (Rafles 1978).

10. ≠ indicates difference; I shows the homology between components exactly above and below this sign.

Table 1. Correspondences in Javanese classification sets.

Set	Correspondence				
	I	II	III	IV	V
Market day	*Legi*	*Paing*	*Pon*	*Wage*	*Kliwon*
Colour	White	Red	Yellow	Black	Multi-coloured
Cardinal point	East	South	West	North	Centre
Kinship Relation	*Kaki* (grand-father)	*Nini* (grand-mother)	*Bapak* (father)	*Ibu* (mother)	*Anak* (child)
Characters in the *Tantu Panggelaran*[11]	Mangu-kuhan (farmer)	Sandang-garba (merchant)	Katung-malaras (tapper)	Karung-kalah (butcher)	Wertikan-dayun (king)
Territorial Division	*Manca-negara Negara-gung*	South Java Sea	*Manca-negara Negara-gung*	Mt. Me-rapi.	*Negara Negara*
Quadrant in model	Immanent	Exist-ential	Transcen-dent	Essential	O

11. In this myth Kandihawan was the avatar taken by Vishnu upon being sent down to earth by the god Mahakarana (Mahakarsa) at the time Java was first created. Vishnu was to become the world's teacher and ruler. On this mission he was accompanied by his wife, Sri or Kanyawan, who bore him five sons : Mangukuhan, Sandanggarba, Katungmalaras, Karungkalah, and Wertikandayun. his mission completed, Kandihawan was instructed to appoint one of his sons to act in his stead and return to heaven. As none of the five was willing to assume responsibility for the world, they agreed to draw lots to determine who should replace their father. The choice fell to Wertikandayun, and he became king. Mangukuhan became a farmer and kept the king supplied with food for the rest of life. Sandanggarba was a merchant, and saw to it that the king never lacked for money. Katung-malaras tapped palm trees to make the royal wine. Karungkalah, a butcher. filled the king's table with delectable viands. It should also be mentioned that Kandihawan's sons were also involved with the occurrence of the multi-colour: white, black, yellow and red (Pigeaud 1924 : 60–62) and 132–134: see also Pieaud 1977).

same principle was at work in the territorial division of the kingdom. If this was in fact the case, then the homologous differences between these territories and the cardinal points can be drawn as:

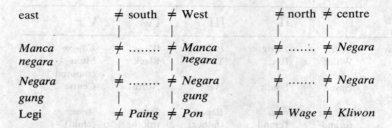

Figure 10. Homology Between Territorial Division and Spacial and Temporal Classifacion Sets.

Thus far I have demonstrated that there are homologies of differences between sets of Javanese classification. In view of the fact that there are fixed correspondences between the positions of components in these sets, one can ask whether it is possible that the Javanese had deduced the homologies between these components [12]. If they had actually done so, than the following classification may very well have existed in the Javanese idea of territorial division:

---

12. K. Miyazaki (1977 : 66–69) argues that there is no maximal correspondence betwen classification sets, i.e. correspondence between components in different sets. However, there is as yet insufficiant proof with which to deny the occurrence of maximal correspondence. Moreover, each position in the model of this classification set can basically be expressed by means of a dichotomy, except for the centre, which tends to be constant. Hence it is conceivable that: *Wage* = north = south; *Legi* = east = west; *Paing* = south = north; and *Pon* = west = east. See Appendix 3 for futher explanation.

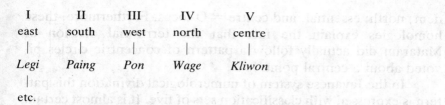

I	II	III	IV	V
east	south	west	north	centre
Legi	*Paing*	*Pon*	*Wage*	*Kliwon*
etc.				

Figure 11. Homology Between Components in Classification Sets.

Pigeaud (1977: 71–72) attempts to explain the possible homology between components in different classification sets by tracing back through certain correspondences. To my way of thinking, his first correspondence relates to the notion of beginning. For example, *wetan*, the Javanese word for east, is derived from *wet* . = beginning of the day; Gana = progenitor of the gods; Mangukuhan (farmer) = first-born son; *Legi* or the day *Umanis* (related to *tis* = cool = morning). Pigeaud's second correspondence involves the association between unfulfilled desires and itinerance, as seen for example in the habits of merchants (Kandihawan's son, Sandanggarba), and *asu ajag* (wolves). The third correspondence encompasses everything giving the impression of being contradictory: pleasure, glory, gold, and Kamajaya (the god of love) but also weakness, illness and misfortune. The fourth relates to the association between regression, death and dejection: Durga (the goddess of death), Karungkalah (butcher), black (sadness) and *Wage* (related to *lawe* or *laweyan,* the name for a much-feared ghost)[13]. The fifth and final correspondence is connected with the idea of permanence and multifariousness: the king, home, Earth, *Kliwon* and multi-colour.

It would not be an overstatement to say that the homologies outlined above are related with the model I have developed. The classification sets have a correspondence with the polar coordinates involving transcendent: immanent and essential: existential in that east: immanent, south: existential, west: transcen-

---

13. In Bagelen it was customary to place the dead on a pallet with the head facing north (Inggris 1921 : 90).

dent, north: essential, and centre = O-locus. Furthermore, these homologies explain the fact that the territorial division of Mataram did actually follow a pattern of concentric circles pivoted about a central point.

In the Javanese system of numerological divination this pattern is expressed with classification sets of five. It is almost certain that the word *mancanegara* was originally connected with a pentadic classification of space such as is found in the system of grouping five villages into one *mancapat* (Moertono 1981: 27). The concept of *mancapat* has also been used to describe the traditional ethic of *rukun* (harmonious co-existence) operating between one village and four others located around it at each cardinal point (Ossenbruggen, 1977).

Bagelen is a classic example of a region having been divided according to the principle of *mancapat*. It was still possible to find *glondongan* administrative units composed of five villages in Bagelen as far into this century as the 1950's (Koentjaraningrat 1964: 160). Clearly then, we can see that as far as territorial organization is concerned, the basic structure of Javanese logic as reflected in the kingship tradition was applied by means of a consistent transformation model, the transformation being done through a numerological classification and appearing at the surface level in the form of *mancapat* and *glondongan* units. It now remains to examine the extent to which the Javanese kingship model of relationships was applied in the organization of rural social relations in Bagelen.

2. Rural Society in Bagelen.

Bagelen's geo-political position within the Mataram king-dom had a marked effect on its social structure. Prior to being signed over to the Dutch in 1830, Bagelen had been part of the *negaragung* and thus parcelled into a great many appanages, the usufruct to which was granted to officials living at the capital. The appanage system was regulated in such a way that no official could ever gain control of any very extensive tract of land[14]. From the point of view of the king such an arrangement was highly desira-ble since it prevented appanage-holders from integrating large units of peasant support which, in the wrong hands, could be turned against himself. Although this system may have been advantageous for the king, it ruptured inter-village integration, separating the interests of one village from those of its neighbours to the point where inter-village warfare became a common occur-rence. (Doorn 1926: 26; Kollman 1864: 354). It was also because of this system that the partition of Bagelen under the Treaty of Gianti had been so haphazard, with villages being indiscrimi-nately allocated to either Surakarta or Yogyakarta simply on the basis of whether they fell within the appanage of an official from the first or second court.

It is difficult to find detailed maps showing the territories of both courts, especially those holdings under wet-rice cultivation in lowland areas, such as Purworejo, Kutoarjo and Kebumen. On de Klerck's map (Appendix 2) a large slice of southern Bagelen is re-presented as one unit belonging to both Surakarta and Yogyakar-ta with no details as to who actually owned what. Table 2 provides a list of territories belonging to either of the two courts (Kollman 1864: 358), but it should be noted that these units are still only rough approximations (Doorn 1926: 19).

---

14. This was usually done by limiting the number of *cacah* (peasant house-holds) farming appanage lands by means of the *pancasan* system (Ongho-kham 1977 : 619). Cf. chapter II.4 footnote 33.

Table 2. Allocation of districts in Bagelen[15]

	Mahosan dalem	Lungguh	Kerja gladak
Surakarta:			
	1. Tanggung (Cangkrep,	2. Merden (Kebumen)	1. Gesikan (Kutoarjo)
	2. Wala (Ambal, Kutoarjo)	2. Kutowinangun	
	3. Panjer (Kebumen)		
	4. Tlaga		
Yogyakarta.			
	1. Bapangan (Jenar, Purworejo)	1. Loano (Purworejo)	1. Selomerto
	2. Semawung (Kutoarjo)	2. Blimbing (Karanganyar)	
	3. Ngrawa	3. Roma Jatinegoro (Karanganyar)	
	4. Watulembu		
	5. Lengis (Kutoarjo)		
	6. Selomanik (Wonosobo)		
	7. Semaiju (Wonosobo)		

15. Holdings administered by Surakarta and Yogyakarta comprised :
    1) *mahosan dalem,* or crownlands; 2) *lungguh,* or appanages reserved for officials; 3) *kerja gladak or, holdings from which corvée labour was drawn for work in the place or royal forests; 4) lands set aside for religious institutions, ecclesiastics and cemetary custodians, and considered sacred (Doorn 1926 : 17).*

From the facts just presented it will be evident that pre-colonial (until 1830) Bagelen society was too fragmented to have constituted an integrated structure under one rule encompassing the entire region. There are three reasons for this; the first two are quite straightforward, the third requires some explanation. First, Bagelen could hardly have been integrated while under the administration of two separate kings. Second, the territorial jurisdiction of both rulers was so interjacent that any geo-political representation of Bagelen could not help but be likened to a mosaic. Third, both rulers had delegated their authority over the various fragments of Bagelen to more than one person.

In pre-colonial times it was the king's practice to appoint a minister known as a *priyayi gunung* to administer policy and civil justice in the districts listed in Table 2; Bagelen had one such minister from Yogyakarta and three from Surakarta (TNI 1858: 76). They recieved a salary in praedial tithes collected from peasants on their appanages. Their position was comparable to that of a regent, the main difference being that *priyayi gunung* were not authorized to handle the finances and taxation of the area under their administration; this task was assigned to *priyayi patuh* who resided in the capital[16]. Both *priyayi gunung* and *priyayi patuh* would then delegate their authority to *demang* (district functionaries), who would in turn delegate theirs to *bekel* (tax-collectors). This parcelling out of authority was usually arranged on a rational profit and loss basis. As one of the main aspects of authority had to do with tax collection, or the accumulation of materiality, high-level functionaries tended to auction off their authority, so to speak, to the highest bidder, i.e., those guaranteeing to collect the most taxes. It was precisely this model of rational profit and loss relations which led tax-collectors into the

---

16. The manner in which royal authority was delegated differed greatly between the *negaragung* and *mancanegara*. Regents in the *mancanegara* had complete sovereignty over their territory and were required only to make annual tribute payments to the king. They were, in short, small-scale kings, or a transformation of the king in miniature.

practice of siphoning off excessive amounts of material resources from those in subordinate positions.[17] Moreover, the arbitrariness of their levies and harshness of their collection techniques increased with their distance away from the watchful eye of the palace (TNI 1858: 73). Proof of the extraordinarily heavy drain on peasant income is evinced in the number and diversity of taxes listed below (TNI 1858: 77–78):

1. Land tax or rents, including a head tax levied by the village administrator.
2. *Takker turun:* state requisitions equivalent to a tax. These were designed to cover the material and labour needs of the king or appanage-holder. Produce, goods and corvée were requisitioned in such a way than no village would ever have had to supply all three on any one occasion.
3. *Kirjaji (kirgaji):* annual land cesses amounting to 24 *ketip* (1 *ketip* = 10 cents) per *jung* (28,386 m²), one half of which was used to pay the salaries of *priyayi gunung,* with the balance going for unkeep to bridges on main roads.
4. *Pacunplang (pacumplang):* a tax of one gulden per *jung* for purchasing cotton yarn for the royal looms.
5. *Uang bekti* or *uang panjaran:* fees for service paid by lower to higher functionaries as a token of their loyalty and appreciation for having been given their position. These were not fixed in amount but collected as a matter of course whenever there was a change of functionary. Thus, for each new *demang* or *bekel* there was another patronage appointment for the peasants to finance.
6. *Pasumbang:* contributions of 30 *sen* (cents) per *jung* to defray the cost of staging palace wedding feasts.

---

17. *Bekel,* for example, took 20 times more in taxes than they were required to hand over to superiors, besides which they also demanded corvée for miscellaneous purposes of their own devising (Doorn 1926 : 28).

7. *Pajindralan:* contibutions of 30 *sen* per *jung* for banquets held during the Dutch governor-general's visits to the courts of Surakarta or Yogyakarta.
8. *Peniti:* census fees of one *duit* per capita.
9. *Bijigar:* livestock inventory fees of one *spaanschemat* (Spanish dollar = 2.50 gulden) per cow or water buffalo. The purpose of the inventory was to assess how much stock a functionary could later requisition.
10. *Uborompo (ubarampe):* a levy of 15–30 *ketip* per *jung* used to buy cakes and other food which village administrators were obliged to bring along when making obeisance to the courts at Surakarta or Yogyakarta.
11. *Pakuning:* rents on wet-rice land paid to administrators in certain villages.
12. *Pa-iring:* cash rents paid by non-residents to the village administrator for the privilage of bringing their wet-rice crop to harvest. Payment amounted to half a year's rent and was due before the rice was ripe and ready for sale.
13. *Pundutan:* contingency levies issued by the village administrator for purchasing horses and clothing, and for paying his own fines.

Judging from the size of the material burden imposed upon the peasantry from above, the position of *priyayi* in the Javanese kingship model would be close to the maximum immanent-existential indicator, which means that it was no longer in accordance with the model of the *kawula-Gusti* relationship which Javanese leaders were ideally supposed to emulate. In order to adjust this position, the *priyayi* began to imitate the life style of the king. One finds many instances in historical writings[18] to support this statement. Middle- and lower-level functionaries built up social circles in their own locality and in territories under their control based on models developed by the king. And even though the

18. See for example Sutjipto (1980 : 7); Sutherland (1979); Onghokham (1975); Geertz (1983 : 305–344); and Burger (1939).

kawula-Gusti model was not always ideal, the *priyayi* applied it anyway in order to sustain their relationship with those under them. In fact, it would be possible to write a whole book on the transformation of the kingship model along the line showing the heirarchy of the king's authority based on the habits of the *priyayi* alone. They wrote their own family myths, compiled fictitious genealogies, built up a collection of fetishtic *pusaka,* and performed ceremonies intended to bring them into contact with supernatural forces, all of which represented ways of legitimating their position in society. The following myth, taken from the *Danurejo Book of Genealogy*[19] , is intended by way of an example of how Bagelen *priyayi* legitimated their position. The myth is a typical rags-to-riches story of a young boy who starts out as a humble gatherer of wood and ends up becoming a *priyayi gunung.*

> The sage Raden Panulahar having decided to change his place of meditation left Tugarana Hill in the Wirasaba district and went to Wulan Hill. This new retreat, in Roma Gombong, was known by the name of Gergeng. Here the sage stayed inside the hollow trunk of Kroya Growong, the honourable banyan tree. As well-concealed as this remote retreat was, a young boy, Bagus Janah, accidently learned of its whereabouts.
>
> Bagus Janah's father was Kyai (the Venerable) Buyut Kuwu Ngrawa, a descendent of Kyai Ageng Getas Pandawa Pakis-aji through Kyai Ageng Ngabdulrahman in Ela, Nyai Ageng Sikap, Kyai Ageng Benco buried in Roma, and Kuwu Benco. The boy himself was fond of making ascetic retreats in lofty places. On this particular day he had come to the foot of Wulan Hill to collect dry wood. Reaching the northwest side of the hill, he began following a muddy track leading up to a spring. That was where he first sighted the *Kawo,* a guana of large proportions and great age. He pursued the guana further up the hill, going deeper and deeper into the forest until the trees grew so thickly together that the way became impassable. The guana slipped off through a space in a tangle of lianas, leaving Bagus alone and completely lost under the canopy of the stately Kroya Growong. The boy then remembered that dank, secluded places such as this were the favorite haunts of the rhinoceros, wild buffalo and python. His fear grew as he noticed a charred circle in a place where no human should have been. Not long afterwards the maker of the fire stepped out from among the trees as if from nowhere. He was dressed in a simple robe over loose trousers and an *udeng*

19. The complete title of the book is: *Salasilahing Para Leluhur ing Kadenurejan* (Lor 6686-H-23.960).

77

(traditional Javanese headgear) such as ascetics were want to wear. Seeing Bagus' footprints in the soft ground, he knew that someone had discovered his retreat. He shouted, "Trespasser! Leave this place at once" The boy walked over to where the voice had come from, but there was no one there—the sage was already back inside the banyan tree. He called out politely and the sage's voice echoed from within the tree: "Be still out there! I am having a vision. You outside! You are destined to become the founder of this district and leader of a village. You will father a line of great leaders. It will be no easy task to fulfil your destiny. I can tell you no more, save that if you follow the mashy trail leading down from the spring, you will find something to help you."

On hearing the sage's words the happy boy set off to do as he was bid. He was still looking for the place the sage had directed him to when Ketip Kuning and Santri Gudig came by. They were the sage's pupils and had been instructed to bring back something hidden in a pool of white stone at the foot of Wulan Hill. When the two novices looked into the pool, all they could see was a common *gabus* fish. They returned to the sage saying they had seen nothing but a fish. The sage again instructed them to bring back whatever was in the pool. Back they went and after some time returned, carrying the fish, which had all the while been trying to squirm out of their grasp.

The moment the sage touched the fish, it changed into the rippling blade of a *keris* (dagger) encased in a sheath. The sage opened the sheath and presented Bagus Janah with the weapon, telling him to use it well. He prophesied that whoever wore the *keris* would be able to safeguard Javanese leadership.

After this the sage moved on to Cikanco Hill in Ngayah where he became a great religious teacher. He was so much respected by the local people that they gave him the name Raden Jaka Krenda Arya Panulahar. Not long afterwards Bagus Janah helped the Sultan of Pajang put down a village rebellion in Sarawindu in Medangkele, Bagelen and he, too, was rewarded with a new name: Adipatih Janah, Regent of Kapucang, in charge of the whole district of Roma .... (Lor 6686- H- 23- 960 pp. 24- 27).

For all that the Janah Bagus myth is like a half-remembered scent teasing the memory with snatches of déjà vu, the main image to focus on is that of a temporal leader looking to the transcendental power of a religious sage and magical *keris* for support. It should also be noted that it was Bagus Janah's ascesis, or world-renunciation, which attracted this transcendental power to him. In the myth, Adipatih Janah's position was oriented not merely towards temporal power, i.e., putting down a peasant revolt, but also towards his union with forces of a transcendental nature. Thus, one could say that through this myth some, but not all, aspects of the kingship model were applied in order to legitimate the *priyayi* position on the hierarchical scale of the king's authority.

As regards rural society in Bagelen, there is very little in the way of documentation aside from records dealing with the administration of Mataram, and these mainly provide details of the hierarchy and distribution of authority throughout the kingdom. It is for this reason that any researcher attemping a re-construction of pre-colonial society must be wary of reducing this society to a network of relations based around resource management. As the management of any resource always implies the direction and regulation of manpower, there may be a tendency to regard rural society as little other than a group of peasants interwoven by the kingdom's control over their persons and means of production. From this perspective, discrete members of rural society would certainly not be integrated with one another, apart from the fact that all paid taxes to the *bekel* and *demang* who, according to the existing administrative channels, were their superiors. And, since there has never been a society (even a communist one) which operated on the basis of an ideal distribution model, i.e., a fair and equal division of all material resources, a resource management approach could very easily lead one to the narrow view of rural society as a stratified class society.

I do not doubt for a moment that the surface of rural society was streaked through with various striae of relationships. A number of different studies have shown that there were at least two broad classes in pre-colonial rural society: the *sikep*, who controlled arable land, and the landless labourers who lived by tilling the *sikep*'s fields (Breman 1980: 21–27; Onghokham 1977: 620; Hugenholtz 1983: 25). It may be possible to break these two classes into even smaller ones. Kollman (1864: 366–367) tried to reconstruct the social stratification of rural Bagelen in pre-colonial times on the basis of retrospective interviews. His data may be somewhat unreliable, however, because his informants do not appear to remember much about Bagelen before 1830; consequently their descriptions are more representative of social conditions in the 1860's. Kollman's version of social stratification in rural Bagelen, excluding the position of village administrators runs as follows:

1. *Kuli baku:*those owning irrigated-rice fields and compounds who were required to perform full corvée service for others in superior positions of control over land (administrators).
2. *Lindung:* those with a house and compound but no fields of their own.
3. *Pondok* or *numpang:* those with no fields and no compound. They usually shared the *kuli baku*'s compound and provided corvée only for public works projects. There were two types of *pondok: pondok tempel* and *pondok slusub.* The former had his own house on the *kuli baku*'s compound; the latter roomed with the *kuli baku* but was not given board.
4. *Rayat:* those rooming and boarding with the *kuli baku* and helping with any work undertaken.

In this description, rural society takes on the appearance of a graduated configuration with land ownership as the determining factor. However, such a configuration is only partially representative of rural social struture because differing degrees of control over material (land) resources were not particularly conducive to the growth of inter-class collective solidarity. In fact, it is precisely such differences which would have tended to compartmentalize villagers and orient them away from, rather than in the direction of, integration. In reality, there were a good number of village activities which may be very difficult to visualize, but did nevertheless, promote the feeling of solidarity, and were intended to encourage social integration. Before discussing the exact nature of these activities I would like to draw attention to some of Robert Jay's remarks on Mojokuto society.

Robert Jay (1969: 281–188) observes that at a higher level of abstraction Mojokuto people tend to conceive of their society as an undifferentiated mass, and avoid any overt reference to personal rank[19]. Differences in personal rank are transformed into a gesture concealed within actual social relations. This means that the expression of one's own rank, that of the person addressed, and that of the person referred to, depends upon the context of the social relation, which varies for each of the individuals concerned. Rank, then, is conveyed through an exchange of gestures indicating the relative social position of each individual within the social event[20]. It is through gestures containing this social evaluation that the Javanese attempt to determine one another's position as accurately as possible at the time the actual social relations are in progress. A good example of how this works is the selection of lexical items from speech levels when engaging in social intercourse.

The three main speech levels in Javanese, i.e., *ngoko, madya,* and *kromo,* are marked by differences in lexical items and affixes (Poedjosoedarmo 1968: 57). The *ngoko* lexicon is informal and generally not considered elevated enough for the formal presentation of self in society. The *madya* lexicon is used to address people with whom one is well-acquainted, such as older relatives, as this adds just the right touch of rather formal politeness required by the relationship. The *kromo* lexicon is the appropriate choice when addressing people with whom it is necessary to be formal and socially distant. The fact that Javanese contains these speech levels means that speakers must select for a definite code[21] in order to respond to the social event in which they are participating. The choice of lexicon also conveys information about the speaker's own position, that of the addressee, and that of the refe-

---

19. Personal rank refers to the evaluation of an individual's qualities as made by others on the basis of existing social values (Jay 1969 : 281).
20. Jay uses the concept of situational rank to express the relative positions of each person within the social event (1969 : 281).
21. For a discussion of codes see John. U. Wolff and S. Poedjosoedarmo (1982).

rent within the context of that particular event. If the speaker opts for a *ngoko* code he establishes that his position is higher than, or on a par with, that of the addressee; a *madya* code shows that his position is slightly below the addressee's; a *kromo* code indicates that the addressee's position is high while his own is much lower. Besides establishing the individual's situational rank, the choice of speech levels also determines the degree of intimacy which is desirable for the particular event. This is an important factor because intimacy tends to take precedence over personal rank. If, however, both speakers are using different speech levels, rank tends to outweigh intimacy.

This brief description should serve to illustrate that there are very complex relationships in rural society. Javanese social structure cannot be reduced to that of a stratified class society because the Javanese acknowledge logical processes which view their society as an undifferentiated social mass, in spite of the fact that they also acknowledge differences in personal rank. The first logical process equalizes each villager's position and thus provides an opportunity for the growth of familiarity leading to collective solidarity.

The basis for this feeling of solidarity is, then, a logic system which organizes the components it encompasses according to the principle of identical positioning (page 7). This means that in real-life activities villagers classify one another within a framework of equality, and view the position of others as equal or identical to their own according to the context. There is very little proof of a logic system emphasising identical positioning during the pre-colonial period. As mentioned before, most records deal with the running of a polity concerned with the accumulation of power and materiality. But a logic system based on a framework of identical positioning is more inclined towards the renunciation of material accumulation, i.e., ignores personal rank and differences in degree of authority. In terms of the logic model as developed throughout this discourse, such a system is more closely aligned with actions leading to the transcendent-existential quadrant. It would require a complete socio-cultural ethnography to analyse the extent to which this framework of equality contributed to the development of rural society in pre-colonial Bagelen. No such ethnography exists, and to compile one from extant historical data would be a labour far beyond the scope of this work. At most all I can do is to demonstrate that a logic system emphasising equality did in fact exist, and was manifested in rural social life in Bagelen.

That present-day Javanese society acknowledges a logical principle emphasising equality can be seen from Jay's observation that at a certain conceptual level, rural people perceive their society as being undifferentiated. Furthermore such praxis as the *selamatan* are opposed to the principle of caste and hierarchy.

In Clifford Geertz' general description of the *selamatan* as found in Mojokuto (1983: 13–104) one sees that this praxis enhances social integration, particularly along the territorial boundaries of the villages concerned. All the symbols coming to the fore during the *selamatan* represent social unity.i.e.,integration. Participants in this social event: friends, neighbours, and kinsmen, are envisioned as being joined by the spirits of the dead, ancestral spirits and the gods in a simple meal sanctified through prayer. Judging from the range of figures propitiated through the symbols in the offertory ritual, an effort is also made to combine and thus reconcile different religious beliefs. The *selamatan,* therefore, has an integrative function; it symbolizes the mystical and social unity of all who participate in it (Geertz 1983: 13).

While there is little documentation to support the argument that *selamatan* were as much a part of social life in pre-colonial Bagelen as they are elsewhere in Java today, this certainly does not mean that *selamatan* did not exist. Given the nature of records from the pre-colonial period, it is fortunate that any reference to such a non-administrative event should survive at all. One report made in 1846 describes a *selamatan* held before villagers in Karang Bolong left to collect birds' nests (TNI 1846: 313–326). In order to protect the nest-gatherers, a male water buffalo and billy goat were sacrificed; opium and incence were burned; ritual offerings were made to Nyai Rara Kidul and the tutelary spirits of Karang Bolong; and a *wayang* performance was staged. *Selamatan* are also reported to have been held for village purificatory ceremonies (Djawa 1921: 119–120); circumcisions and weddings, and at other critical junctures in life (Inggris 1921: 84–22)[22]. There is also a short description of a mid-twentieth century *selamatan* in Bagelen (Koentjaraningrat 1964: 145–151).

Further evidence of village activities based on the perception that every villager was an identical component of his society is found in references to security arrangements. The *Nawolo Pradoto* mentions that the whole village shared responsibility for the safety of overnight guests. All villagers were liable to a fine in the event that such guests were robbed, injured or murdered during their stay. The fine for guests who died while in the village, for instance, was 50 *rejalen*. The organization of villages into *glondongan* units, which Koentjaraningrat (1964: 160) suggests were similar to *mancapat* villages was, among others, a real activity intended to facilitate inter-village security arrangements.

To summarize briefly then, it can be said that within the framework of Javanese logic, society was not to be structured only by an ethos of materialism, i.e., the accumulation of power and material possessions. There was social stratification because there were differences in personal rank, and the Javanese were most certainly as aware of these as they were of differences in land ownership and control over means of production. Nevertheless, they did not choose to accept these facts as a viable model of their society because for them, the truest model of social relations was the one reflecting the harmonious unity of the *kawula-Gusti* relationship. They also knew that if an individual did not neutralize the accumulation of wealth by redistribution, he alienated himself from the O-locus of the logic model and, by corollary, contradicted the model of *manunggaling kawula-Gusti*. Activities such as the *selamatan,* the traditional ethic of *gotong-royong* (community spirit), and provision for the safety of others were

---

22. See also Moesa (1923 : 128–132).

opposed to the accumulation of materiality and directed towards the development of collective solidarity. Finally, it can be said that the structure of rural society was envisioned in the Javanese mind as a dynamic model gravitating towards its lodestone: *manunggaling kawula-Gusti,* for it was here that the highest ideal in Javanese life was to be found: the harmonic unity of spiritual and material existence (*ketenteraman lahir-batin*).

IV. CONCLUSION

Throughout the various phases of this discussion I have endeavoured to set forth a coherent explanation of Javanese logic as regards the order of society. Within this system of thought Javanese society had a structured orderliness, the dynamics or tradition of which I have described as far as possible, given the constraints on available data. This orderliness is reflected in various traditions found within the milieu of both kingdom and village. Moreover, each facet of this orderliness appears to have a mutual correspondence explainable by means of a model. The correspondences are obtained by crossing the paradoxical features of tradition, which is inherently trancendent and immanent, with reality, which is in practice existential, but in theory, essential. At the intersection of this paradoxical tradition and paradoxical reality is the O-locus, which cannot be classified in the direction of any one pole characterizing the paradoxes. Outside the O-locus there is a clock-wise centripetal cycle (Fig. 4).

While this model may not have been a specific feature of Javanese society, I have attempted to show that it is capable of explaining the complex dynamics of this society because it encompasses the way in which the Javanese perceived reality within the matrix of their social system. This outlook did not just emphasise differences, it also emphasised equivalences, each according to the context. The model also captures the Javanese idea of the tempo of life as a cycle of harmonic change.

Although there was nothing particularly egalitarian about the structure of pre-colonial society, it also cannot be equated with either a class or a caste society. The Javanese acknowledged the stratification and hierarchy of authority present in society but, at the same time, they stated through their traditions that they were-egalitarian. Within such a structure the network of social relations was full of processes to locate the individuals involved according to the context unfolding within the social relation. Hence, an individual's position was not fixed in the temporal continuum just as it was not fixed within the continuum of the social relation.

86

In closing, I would like to add that the study of Javanese social structure requires that one be attentive to the dynamic processes embodied within it. Javanese society can never be explained simply by means of a dualistic classification involving closed pairs of binary opposites, such as refined:coarse, élite: masses, rich:poor, because through their ligic system, and social practices and activities, the Javanese showed that they did not accept such a classification as being the truest for their society.

BIBLIOGRAPHY

Anderson, B.R.O'G, 1965, *Mythology and the Tolerance of the Javanese.* Monograph Series. Ithaca, New York: Modern Indonesia Project Southeast Asia Program, Department of Asian Studies Cornell University.

——, 1972. "The idea of Power in Javanese Culture" in Claire Holt (ed), *Culture and Politics in Indonesia,* Ithaca, Cornell University Press, 1972, pp. 1–69.

ARA 6488, 507, *Ministerie can Kolonien Mailrapporten 1981. Summary of Policy Decisions by Netherlands East Indies Govermen-General on Emigration from Bagelen to Priangan.*

Berg, C.C., 1938. *"De Arjuna Wiwaha, Er-Langga's Levensloop en Bruilofslied?",* in *BKI,* No. 93 pp. 19-93.

——, 1938a "Javaansche geschciedschrijving", in *Geschiedenis van Nederlandsch Indie.* F.W. Stapel, Amsterdam Deel II, pp. 5-148.

Boediardjo, 1978. "Wayang: A Reflection of the Aspirations of the Javanese", in *Dynamics of Indonesian History.* Haryati Soebadio and C.A du Marchie Sarvaas (eds). Amsterdam, New York, and Oxford: North-Holland Publishing Company. pp. 97-121.

Booke, J.H., 1910. *Tropische-Koloniale Stadhuishoudkunde.* Dissertation, Amsterdam.

Bosch, F.D.K., 1956. "C.C Berg and Ancient Javanese History", in *BKI (Bijdragen tot de Taal, Land, en Volkenkunde).* 112, pp. 1-24.

Bratakesawa, R., 1952. *Katrangan Tjandrasangkala Djakarta: Balai Pustaka. ('28)*

Breman, J., 1980. *The Village on Java and the Early-Colonial State.* Rotterdam: The Comparative Asian Studies Programme (CASP).

Burger, D.H., 1939. *De Onsluiting van Java's Binnenland Voor Het Werelderkeer.* Dissertation. Wageningen: H. Veenman Zonen.

88

——, 1957 *Structural Changes in Javanese Society: The Village Sphere.* Ithaca: Modern Indonesia Project.

——, 1975 *Sociologisch-Economische Geschiedenis van Indonesia.* Deel I, Wageningen, Amsterdam, Leiden.

Carey, P.B.R., 1974. "Javanese Histories of Diponegoro: The Buku Kedhung Kebo. Its Authorship and Historical Importance", *Bijdragen tot de Tall –, Land –, en Volkenkunde.* Deel 130. pp. 259-288.

——, 1976. "The Origins of the Java War (1825-30)", *The English Historical Review.* Vol XCI Longmans (Quarterly). January 1976, No. CCCL VIII pp. 52-78.

——, 1979. "Aspects of Javanese History in the Nineteenth Century", in Harry Aveling (ed). *The Development of Indonesian Society from the Coming of Islam to the Present* Day. St. Lucia: University of Queensland Press. pp. 45-105.

——, 1981. *Waiting for The Ratu Adil ("Just King"): The Javanese Village Community on the Eve of Java War (1825-30).* Paper to be presented at the Second Anglo-Dutch Conference on Comparative Colonial History, Leiden.

de Graaf, H.J., 1949. *Geschiedenis van Indonesie.* S-Gravenhage.

——, 1970. "Sejarah Pangiwa lan Panengen", *BKI* No. 126. pp. 332-337.

de Jong, 1976. *Salah Satu Sikap Hidup Orang Jawa.* Yogyakarta: Yayasan Kanisius Press.

de Josselin de Jong, P.E., 1977 "The Participants' View of Their Culture", in *Structural Anthropology in the Netherlands.* P.E. de Josselin de Jong (ed). The Hague: Martinus Nijhoff.

de Ruijter, A., 1977. *Claude Lévi-Strauss, Een Systeemanalyse van zijn Anthropologish Werk.* Dissertation-ICAU mededeling No. 11 Utrecht.

——, 1981. "Structural Anthropology in the Netherlands in the Nineteen Seventies", in *Current Issues in Anthropology: the Netherlands.* Peter Kloos and H.J.M Claessen (eds). Rotterdam: Anthropological Branch of the Netherlands

89

Sociological and Anthropological Society. pp. 191-199.

Dewantara, Ki Hadjar, 1967. *Kebudayaan.* Part IIA, Jogjakarta: Majelis Luhur Persatuan Taman Siswa. p. 32.

Dewey, Alice G, 1962. *Peasant Marketing in Java.* New York: The Free Press of Glencoe, Inc.

Djajadiningrat, Hoesein, Raden, 1913. *Critische Beschouwing van de Sedjarah Banten. Bijdrage ten kenschetsing van de Javaansche Geschiedschrijving. Haarlem : J Enschedé en zonen.*

Djawa, 1921. *"Iets over het Leven van de Veehoeders (Botjah Angon) in het District Krakal Afdeeling Keboemen." Djawa* Jaargang 1. pp. 119-120.

Doorn, C.L. van, 1926. *Schets van de Economische Ontwikkeling der Afdeeling Poerworedjo (Residentie Kedoe).* Weltevreden: G. Kolffs Co.

Drewes, G.W.J., 1925. *Drie Javansche Goeroe's.* Dissertation. Leiden: Drukkerij A. Vros.

Dumont, Louis, 1970. *Homo Hierarchicus. The Caste System and Its Implications,* Chicago: The University of Chicago Press.

Elson, R.E., 1978. *The Cultivation System and "Agricultural Involution."* Working Paper Monash University 14. Melbourne.

ENI, 1971. *Encyclopaedie van Nederlandsch-Indie.* Tweede druk. J. Paulus (ed). S-Gravenhage and Leiden Martinus Nijhoff and N.V v/H E. J. Brill.

Geerts, C., 1963. *Agricultural Involution.* Berkeley, Los Angeles and London: University of California Press.

——, 1983, *Abangan, Santri, Priyayi Dalam Masyarakat Jawa.* Translation. Jakarta: Pustaka Jaya.

Groneman, Cf. J., 1895, *De Garebegs in Yogyakarta.* The Hague: Martinus Nijhoff. p. 35.

Hayes, N.E. and T. Hayes (ed.), 1970. *Claude Lévi-Strauss: The Anthropologist as Hero.* Cambridge: The MIT Press.

Heesterman, C.J., 1985 The Inner Conflict of Tradition. Essays in Indian Ritual, Kingship, and Society. Chicago and London: The University of Chicago Press.

Heine-Geldern, Robert, 1956. *Conceptions of State And Kingship in Southeast Asia*. Data Paper: Number 18 Ithaca New York: Southeast Asia Program, Department of Asian Studies. Cornell University.

Hugenholtz, W.R., 1983. *Traditional Javanese Society and the Colonial Exploitation System: Regional Differences in the Appropriate Principalities in 1830*. Yogyakarta: The Fourth Indonesian-Dutch History Conference 24 th – 29 th July 1983.

Inggris, 1921. "Volksgewoonten in Bagelen", *Djawa*, No. 1. pp. 89-21

——, 1923. "Het Roewatanfeest in de Desa Karangjati in Bagelen", *Djawa*. Derde Jaargang. pp. 45-50.

Jay, Robert R. 1969. *Javanese Villagers' Social Relations in Rural Modjokuto*. Cambridge, Massachusetts, and London: The MIT Press.

Kano, Hiroyoshi., 1980. "The Economic History of Javanese Rural Society: A Reinterpretation" in *The Developing Economies*. Vol XVIII. 1, pp. 3-22.

Kartodirjo, A. Sartono., 1969. "Struktur Sosial dari Masyarakat Tradisionil dan Kolonial," in *Lembaran Sejarah*. December 1969, No. 4.

——, 1970. *Religious Movements of Java in The 19th and 20th Centuries*. Yogyakarta: Faculty of Arts, Gadjah Mada University.

Klerck, E.S. de., 1909. *De Java-Oorlog van 1825-30*. Zesde Deel. Hage: M. Nijhoff

Koentjaraningrat, R.M., 1957. *A Preliminary Description of the Javanese Kinship System*. Yale University Southeast Asia Studies Cultural Report Series.

——, 1964. "Tjelapar: Sebuah Desa di Djawa Tengah Bagian Selatan", in *Masyarakat Desa di Indonesia Masa Ini*. Koentjaraningrat (ed). Djakarta: Jajasan Badan Press, Faculty of Economics, University of Indonesia.

Kollmann, M.H.J., 1864. "Bagelen onder het Bestuur van Soera-karta en Djokjakarta", in *Bataviaasch Genootschap van Kunst en Wetenschappen* (TBG). Deel XIV pp. 352-368.

Labberton, D. Van Hinlopen., 1921. "Oud Javansche Gegevens Omtrent de Vulkanalogie van Java", *Djawa*. Jaargang 1. p. 200.

Lévi-Strauss, C., 1963. *Structural Anthropology*, New York: Basic books.

——, 1966. *The Savage Mind*. London : The University of Chicago press.

Locher, G.W., 1978. *Transformation And Tradition*. Translation Series 18 KITLV. The Hague: Martinus Nijhoff. Chapter VII, IX, X.

Lor 6686-H-23960. *Serat Salasilahing para Loeloehoer ing Kadanoeredjan*. Leiden University Oriental Manuscript.

Louw, P.J.F. dan E.S. de Klerck., 1894–1909. *De Java Oorlog*. Batavia and Den-Haag. Louw in Vol. I to III; and Klerck in Vol IV to VI.

Macklin, B.J and Crumrine, N. Roos., 1974. "Sacred Ritual and the Structure in North Mexican Folk Saints Cults and General Ceremonialism", in *The Unconscious in Culture*. I. Rossi (ed). New York: Dutton & Co; Inc. pp. 179-197.

Majalah Mahasiswa Driyarkara S.T.F "Driyarkara" Jakarta., *Dari Sudut-Sudut Filsafat*. Yogyakarta: Yayasan Kanisius Press.

Miyazaki, K., 1977. *The Problem of "Maximal Correspondence"* ICA Publication No. 35. Leiden: Institute of Cultural and Social Studies, Leiden University.

Moertono, Soemarsaid., 1981. *State and Statecraft in Old Java. A Study of Later Mataram Period, 16th to 19th Century*. Monograph Series (Publication No. 43). Ithaca, New York: Cornell Modern Indonesia Project Southeast Asia Program, Cornell University.

Moesa., 1923. "Onuitwischbore Sporen uit den voor Mohammedaanschen Tijd", in *Djawa*. Jaargang III. pp. 128-132.

92

Monnier, D.L., 1844. "Het Boek der Nawolo Pradhoto" in *Tijdschrift voor Nederlandsch Indie*. 6-I. pp. 247-352.

Moelyono, Sri., 1977. *Wayang dan Karakter Manusia*. (Jakarta): Yayasan Nawangi Pt. Inaltu.

——, 1978. *(a) Wayang Asal-Usul Filsafat dan Masa Depannya*. Jakarta

——, 1978. *(b) Apa dan Siapa Semar*. Jakarta: Gunung Agung.

——, 1974. *Simbolisme dan Mistikisme dalam Wayang*. Jakarta: P.T. Gunung Agung.

Onghokham., 1975. *The Residency of Madiun : Priyayi and Peasant in the Nineteenth Century*. Dissertation, Manuscript.

——, 1979. "Social Change In Madiun (East Java) During the Nineteenth Century : Taxes and Its Influence on Landholding", *Proceedings 7ᵗʰ IAHA Conf. Bangkok 1977*. Bangkok, Vol. I pp. 616-641.

Ossenbruggen, F.D. van., 1977. "Java's monca-pat : Origins of a Primitive Classification System", in *Structural Anthropology in the Netherlands*, P.E de Josselin de Jong (ed). The Hague : Martinus Nijhoff. pp. 30-60.

Pigeaud, Th.G.Th., 1942. *De Tantu Panggelaran*. Dissertation. Leiden University, S-Gravenhage : Nederl-Boek-En steendrukkherij voorheen H. L Smiths.

——, 1927. "Alexander Sakendher en Senopati", *Djawa*. Jaargang VII. pp. 321-381.

——, 1967. *Literature of Java*. Vol. I, pp. 7-9.

——, 1977. "Javanese Divination and Classification", in *Structural Anthropology in the Netherlands. P.E de Josselin de Jong. The Hague : Martinus Nijhoff, pp. 61-82*.

Poedjosoedarmo, Soepomo., 1968. "Javanese Speech Levels", *in Indonesia*. No. 6 (October 1968). pp. 54-81.

Poel, A. van de., 1846. "Oorsprong van den Naam Bagelen". *Tijdschrift voor Nederland's Indie*. Jaargang VIII, deel 3 pp. 173-180.

Poerwodarminto, W.J.S., 1939. *Baoesastra Djawa*. Groningen Batavia : J.B Wolters.

Pouwer, Jan., 1974. "The Structural-Configurational Approach :
A Methodological Outline", in *The Unconscious in Culture*.
Inno Rossi (ed). New York : E.P. Dutton & Co., Inc. pp.
233-255.

Putnam, H., 1978. "Three-Valued Logics", in *Contemporary Philosophical Logic*. New York : St. Martin's Press. pp. 327-334

Raffles, T.S., 1978. *The History of Java*. London : Oxford University Press.

Ricklefs, M.C., 1972. "A Consideration of Three Versions of The
Babad Tanah Djawi. With Excerpts on The Fall of Madjapahit", *Bulletin of The School of Oriental and African Studies*. University of London, Vol 35. Part 2 pp. 285-315.

——, 1973. *Jogjakarta Under Sultan Mangkubumi 1749-1792 : A
History of the Division of Java* (two parts).
Ann Arbor, Michigan and London University Microfilm,
International. Dissertation.

——, 1974. "Dipanegara's Early Inspirational Experience", in
Bijdragen Tot de Taal - Land-en Volkenkunde Deel 130. pp.
227-258.

Ricoeur, Paul., 1978. *Main Trends in Philosophy*. New York,
London : Holmes & Meier Publishers, Inc.

Rosser, J.B. and A.R. Torquette., 1978. "Many-Valued Logics",
in *Contemporary Philosophical Logic*. New York : St. Martin's Press pp. 319-326.

Rossi, Inno., 1974. "Structuralism as Scientific Method"
The Unconscious in Culture. New York : E.P Dutton & Co,
Inc. pp. 60-106.

Rouffaer, G.P., 1931. *Vorstenlanden*. Overdruk uit Adatrechtbundel XXXIV, Series D, No. 81, pp. 233-378.

Sagimun M.D., 1960. *Pahlawan Diponegoro Berjuang (Bara Api
Kemerdekaan nan tak Kunjung Padam)*. Jogjakarta : Tjabang Bagian Bahasa Djawatan Kebudayaan Kem. P.P.K.

——, 1976. *Pahlawan Nasional Pangeran Diponegoro*. Jakarta :
Proyek Biografi Pahlawan. Nasional Dept. of Education
and Culture.

Setiadijaya, Barlan., 1983. "Numerologi Indonesia Ditinjau dari Asas Harmoni Pythagoras", *Kompas*. Week 17 April 1983. p. 8 col. 6-9; and p. 10, col 1-3.

Schriehe, B., 1957. *Ruler and Realm in Early Java*. Selected writings (part two), Den Haag.

Sievers, Allen M., 1974. *The Mystical World of Indonesia, Culture & Economic Development in Conflict*. Baltimore and London: The Johns Hopkins University Press.

Soekanto., 1952. *Sekitar Yogyakarta, 1755-1825* (Perjanjian Gianti-Perang Diponegoro). Djakarta.

Soemardjan, Selo., 1981. *Perubahan Sosial di Yogyakarta*. Yogyakarta : Gadjah Mada University Press.

Spradley, J.P and David McCurdy., 1980. "Culture and the Contemporary World" in *Conformity and Conflict Readings in Cultural Anthropology*. J.P Spradley and D. McCurdy (ed). Boston and Toronto : Little, Brown and Company.

Srinivas, M.N., 1966. *Social Change in Modern India*. Berkeley and Los Angeles : University of California Press.

Stuterheim, W.F., 1931. "The Meaning of the Hindu Javanese Candi", *Journal of the American Oriental Society*. Vol. 51, No. 1, pp. 1-15.

Susanto, Budi., 1977. "Hidup Bahagia Orang Jawa Serat Wedhatama Sebuah Contoh", in *Dari Sudut-Sudut Filsafat*. Majalah Mahasiswa Driyarkara S.T.F Driyarkára (collection), Yogyakarta : Yayasan Kanisius Press, pp. 27-37.

Sutherland, Heather., 1979. *The Making of Bureaucratic Elites : The Colonial Transformation of the Javanese Priyayi*. Singapore, etc. : Heinemann Educational Books (Asia).

Sutjipto, F.A., 1980. "Struktur Burokrasi Mataram," in *Bacaan Sejarah*. No. 6, March 1980. Yogyakarta : History Dept. Faculty of Arts, Gadjah Mada University.

TNI., 1846. "Beschrijving van Karang Bollong en de Vogelnest Klippen Aldaar", *Tijdschrift voor Nederlandsch Indie*. 8. I. pp. 313-326.

——, 1858. "De Toestand van Bagelen in 1830", *Tijdschrift voor Nederlandsch Indie*. 20st Jaargang II. pp. 65-84.

——, 1860. "Losse Aanteekeningen, Gehouden op Eene Reis Over Java, in 1839", *Tijdschrift voor Nederlandsch Indie* No. 22, I. pp. 201-230.

——, 1862. "Beknopt Overzigt van de Residentie Bagelen", *Tijdschrift voor Nederlandsch Indie.* II, pp. 129-140.

Veth, P.J., 1869. *Aardrijkskundig-Statistisch Woordenboek van Ned-Indie.* Amsterdam : P.N Van Kampen.

White, Benjamin., 1971. "Demand for Labor and Population Growth in Colonial Java", *Human Ecology.* 1. 1. pp. 217-225.

——, 1983. *"Agricultural Involution" and its Critics : Twenty years after Clifford Geertz.* ARD Research Seminars, Institute of Social Studies. The Hague.

Wiryamartana, Kuntara., 1977. "Dalang Karungrungan", in *Dari Sudut-sudut Filsafat.* Majalah Mahasiswa Driyarkara STF Driyarkara, Jakarta. Yogyakarta : Yayasan Kanisius Press.

Wolff, John and Poedjosoedarmo S., 1982. *Communicative Codes in Central Java.* Linguistics Series VIII. Data Paper No. 116. South East Asia Program. Dept. of Asian Studies. Cornell University. Ithaca, New York.

Yamin, Muhammad., 1952. *Sedjarah Peperangan Diponegoro, Pahlawan Kemerdekaan Indonesia.* Djakarta.

Zoetmulder, P.J., 1974. *Kalangwan.* The Hague : Martinus Nijhoff.

——, 1982. *Old Javanese-English Dictionary.* S-Gravenhage : Martinus Nijhoff.

APPENDICES

APPENDIX 1

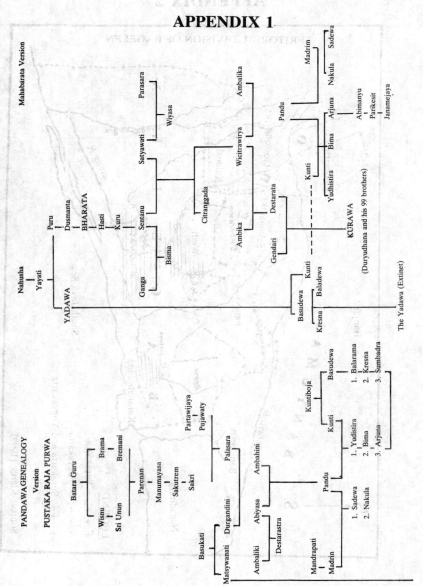

Source : Moelyono (1977)

APPENDIX 2

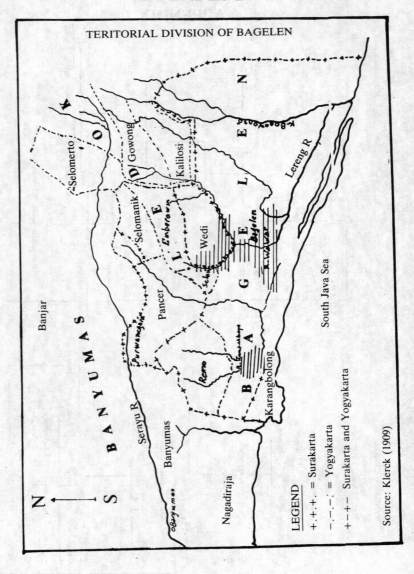

APPENDIX 3

A Note On Maximal Correspondence.

K. Miyazaki (1979 : 66–69) states that there is no maximal correspondence between components in different classification sets. As proof of this, he presents two different *primbon* (divining manuals containing numerological tables, formulae etc. used to make predictions, calculate lucky days, and so on) :

	Primbon I		Primbon II
Wage	= North	=	South
Kliwon	= Centre (all directions)	=	Sky (all directions)
Legi	= East	=	West
Paing	= South	=	North
Pon	= West	=	East

I think that these *primbon* do not adequately substantiate Miyazaki's case against maximal correspondence. Each point is basically multi-directional and can, therefore, be simultaneously classified as north, south, east, west or centre depending on its context and position relative to other points. In terms of the logic model encircling the dynamic at the centre point, each component may occupy a position of opposing directions provided that the centre is stationary. This can be demonstrated as follows:

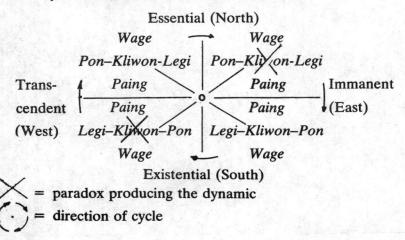

Essential (North)

Existential (South)

$\times$ = paradox producing the dynamic

$(\cdot)$ = direction of cycle

The diagram shows that in the essential quadrant: *Legi* = east, *Paing* = south, *Pon* = west, *Wage* = north and *Kliwon* = centre. However, because of the movement from the essential to existential quadrant following the principle of rotating cycles, it is logical that in the existential quadrant the association will be: *Legi* goes to west, *Paing* to north, *Pon* to east, *Wage* to south, with *Kliwon* still at the centre.

It is probably not simply by chance that the first *primbon* relates more to the essential quadrant; it pertains to astrological numerology which is theoretical (essential) and conservative in nature. On the other hand, the second *primbon* tends to relate to the existential quadrant; it is used for calculating suitable days for journeys, which are associated with change (transience) and, by the same token, with Kandihawan's itinerent son, Sandanggarba, the merchant.

Selected* Glossary Of Non-English Terms

* This list is not exhaustive; terms which occur less frequently, or are peripheral to the core of P.M. Laksono's argument appear in glosses in the text.

babad: chronicles
batin: inner realm of spiritual, emotional and intellectual life.
cacah: peasant households, equal to six persons
demang: district-level functionary
Garebeg: large-scale, public *selamatan* (qv)
glondongan: Administrative unit similar to mancapat (qv)
Gusti: lord, Superior Being, king, authority-figure
Jumbuhing (manunggaling kawula-Gusti): consubstantiation of God and man, unity of king, authority-figure with commoner (see *Gusti*)
kasekten: extraphysical, magical power
kawula: commoner (see *Gusti*)
kejawen: the region of Javanese kingdoms up to the Diponegoro War (1830)
keraton-negara: court, palace-city
lakon: one episode serving as the plot for a single *wayang* performance
mancanegara: wider area of kingdom, extension of *keraton-negaragung* (qv)
mancapat: spacial unit of harmonious co-existence comprising five adjacent villages
negaragung: core area of Mataram, tax field for kingdom's functionaries
panantang: ritual challenge made during investiture of new king
priyayi: officials, middle and lower-level functionaries in kingdom's administrative system
punakawan: comic *wayang* characters thought to symbolize the common man
pusaka: palladia, fetishtic weaponry and state regalia

Ratu Adil: messanianic tradition of the Righteous King
rakyat: the common man, the people
ruwatan: exorcism, disenchantment
santri: orthodox Muslims
satria: knight
selamatan: ritual commensality
suwung-awang-uwung: 'indeterminable' state of emptiness where the self merges with all elements in the cosmos
takdir: predetermination, divine will
titah: fate, divine destiny
tatatentrem: harmonic unity of order between macrocosmos, microcosmos and *batin* (qv)
ulama: Islamic scholars and theologians
wahyu: light of divine favour
wong cilik: commoners, little people

INDEX

106

labuhan 42
lakon 20, 29, 30, 35, 42, 103
lawe 69
laweyan 69

legi 66, 67, 68, 69, 101, 102
Levi-Strauss, C. 5-7, 16, 17, 88, 91
Locher, G.W. 9, 91
Louw, P.J.F. 49, 91
lungguh 62, 72

M

Macklin, B.J. 6, 91
madya 80, 81
Mahabarata 19-21, 23
Mahabarata dan Ramayana 26
mahadewa 33
Mahakarana 67
mahosan dalem 62, 72
Majapahit 19, 43-46
mancanegara 62-64, 70, 73, 103
mancapat 70, 83, 103
maneges karsaning Pangeran 42
manik maya 66
Mangkubumi 48
Mangukuhan 67
manunggaling kawula-Gusti 34, 58
  83, 84
Mas Said 48, 49
Mataram 11, 39, 43, 48, 49, 51, 54,
  59, 62-64, 78
mbaudenda nyakrawati 38
McCurdy, David 10, 94
memangkat 15
menang tanpa ngasorake 36
merapi 43
metaphoric-metonymic 6
Mintarogo 36
Miyazaki, K. 68, 91, 101
model 8, 14, 19, 26-28, 33-36, 47,
  57, 67, 78, 81, 83, 85
momong 15

momot 15
Moertono, Soemarsaid 11-13, 24,
  37-44, 47, 70, 91
Moeljono (Mulyono), Sri 20, 24, 30,
  92, 99
Moesa 83, 91
Monnier, D.L. 92
Mpu Kanwa 55

N

Nahusa 20
Nakula 35
Narada 33
Natakusuma 50
Nawolo Pradoto 83
nayaka 52, 62
negara 62, 63
Negaragung 5, 62-64, 71, 73, 103
neges karsaning pangeran 57
Ngabdulrakhim 56
ngoko 80, 81
Niehoff, Anke XXII
ningrat 45
nini 67
njaba 65
njero 63, 65
nur 37
Nutini 8
Nyai Ageng Sikap 76
Nyai Bagelen 60
Nyai Rara kidul 43, 56, 57, 65,
  82
Nyai Roro Rengganis 60

O

O 35, 41, 43
O-locus 29, 33, 34, 38, 40, 83, 85
Onghokham 2, 3, 50, 71, 75, 78,
  92
Ossenbruggen, F.D. van 70, 92